CONN...

FAMILY ADVENTURE GUIDE™

by

DOE BOYLE

A VOYAGER BOOK

The Globe Pequot Press

OLD SAYBROOK, CONNECTICUT

Family Adventure Guide is a trademark of The Globe Pequot Press, Inc.

Cover and text design by Nancy Freeborn

Library of Congress Cataloging-in-Publication Data
Boyle, Doe.
    Family Adventure Guide : Connecticut / by Doe Boyle. — 1st ed.
       p. cm. — (Family Adventure Guide Series)
    "A voyager book."
    Includes index.
    ISBN 1-56440-646-6
    1. Connecticut—Guide Books. 2. Family recreation—Connecticut—Guidebooks. I. Title. II. Series.
    F92.3.B69   1995
    917.4604'43—dc20   95–13043
                                                   CIP

Manufactured in the United States of America
First Edition/Third Printing

For Tee, who believes it can be done

CONNECTICUT

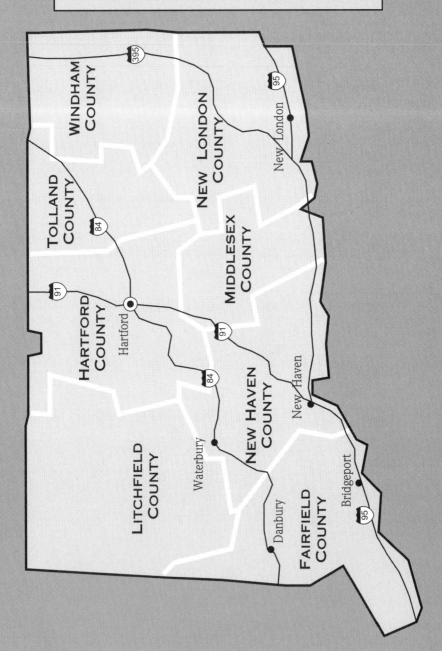

CONTENTS

ACKNOWLEDGMENTS

Many thanks are owed to the scores of people associated with the attractions listed in these pages. Space restraints prevent a listing of their names, but all—from executive director to publicity manager to docent—provided to my family and me a gracious welcome, much information, and the opportunity to enjoy their facilities as "ordinary" families would.

Thanks are also due the individuals at the tourist districts throughout the state. I regret that I cannot name all the people who helped me obtain information, but all were prompt, encouraging, and professional. In particular, Janet Serra of the Litchfield Hills Travel Council, Jennifer Bean of the Greater New Haven Convention and Visitors District, and Diane Moore of the Connecticut Valley District provided cheerful and generous assistance that went well beyond my expectations.

Credit is also due the many dedicated rangers of the Connecticut State Park and Forest system. Every one renewed my faith in the possibility that we can both preserve and protect our land as we educate and entertain our citizens. Every ranger we met was friendly, enthusiastic, and committed to keeping the parks open for family use. I'm happy to report that every one of these knowledgeable and sincere individuals evoked a similar reaction from my children—"Wow, Mom, she (or he) was really nice." No faint praise from a child.

The folks at Globe Pequot Press are owed thanks as well. As an editor, I know that the role of these important players often goes unlauded. The work of Mike Urban, Laura Strom, Mace Lewis, and copy editor Lauren Shafer is in truth as important as my own. I am grateful for their inspiring confidence in my abilities, their patience with the needs of my family, and the freedom they gave me to make the book my own.

I also thank my parents, Gerard and Muriel McDonald, whose role as hostelers was greatly appreciated and vastly underpaid; my niece Ellen, who helped set up campsites in wind and rain and traveled with four children in a car with no stereo, no air conditioning, and no earplugs; and my husband, Tom, who waved goodbye every day and rebuilt our kitchen while we were gone (and who also typed, listened, and loved us all the while).

Most especially, I thank my daughters, without whom there would be no family, no fun, no book. I love you all, most deeply.

INTRODUCTION

In Noah Webster's 1828 *American Dictionary of the English Language,* the word *adventure* is defined, in part, as follows: "an enterprise of hazard; a bold undertaking in which hazards are to be encountered and the issue is staked upon unforseen events." What better description exists of the social phenomenon known as the family daytrip, wherein two or fewer adults headily depart for an outing with an assemblage of one or more children, a map, a travel guide, maybe a camera, a jugful of lemonade, a six-pack of sandwiches, and an abundance of high expectations for fun?

In most families, a variety of ages, interests, and tastes need to be considered at the outset, or the family adventure will threaten to collapse under the weight of varying expectations even before the family car has left the driveway. On some days, simple variables like weather and traffic conspire against the best-laid plans for an enjoyable day.

Perhaps no certain way exists to predict the hazards that may beset your family adventures, but the *Family Adventure Guide: Connecticut* will at least reduce them. Basically, it is a pre-sifted collection of destinations selected by a team of family-fun experts. All the treasures of Connecticut are, in fact, too numerous to be covered in a book this size, and some categories—annual fairs and festivals, for instance—could fill a book of their own. The selection process, therefore, was both objective and subjective. In some cases, inclusion in the book represents a unique or outstanding attraction, superior facilities, or a broad range of appeal. Exclusion, however, does not represent a problem; it usually represents a decision to limit similar attractions within a certain radius or to reduce what might otherwise result in an overemphasis on one category in the book as a whole. Nearly every town in Connecticut, for example, has a wonderful historical society or historic home. Nearly every county has more than one nature center, bird sanctuary, or wildlife preserve. Christmas tree farms and pick-your-own farms are *everywhere* as are toy shops, so-called amusement arcades, and family-friendly eateries. The selection process has resulted in a final list of almost 350 entries, nearly all of which were recently visited by the author and her team of experts. Your team of experts should peruse the options and pick those that suit you and your family best.

You're already a step ahead of many travelers if you've chosen to tour Connecticut or even just one of its counties. The rich history of the region has woven a tapestry of attractions that range from typically Yankee to uniquely sophisticated. Among these pages are boat, train, and trolley rides; science centers and planetariums; canoe trips and river raft races; amusement parks and carousels; both classic and contemporary art museums; zoos; beaches; ski centers; and performing arts of all varieties. There are also many attractions linked to the arts, crafts, and industries of New England: yarn factories, potteries, maple sugar houses, lighthouses, cider mills, and more.

Many attractions reflect Connecticut's remarkable multicultural populations and their histories. Once home to dinosaur and mastodon (both celebrated in some of the state's museums and parks), the prehistoric fertile valleys were later roamed by the nomadic ancestors of the Algonkian people who eventually settled in the gentle hills and along the shores. The Mohican tribe of the Algonkian nation called the region *Quinnehtukqut,* meaning "along the long tidal estuary." The area's indigenous population is represented in many exhibits and festivals throughout the state. At least three museums are dedicated solely to Native American culture.

The arrival of the Dutch in 1614 and the establishment of the Hartford Colony by Englishman Thomas Hooker in 1636 led quickly to the founding of the Connecticut Colony in 1639 and the subsequent decimation of the native population. Despite the shameful nature of that transition, much of value about the European influence can be learned and celebrated in Connecticut today. Wave after wave of immigrants enriched the development of the state and the nation. Patriots, scholars, inventors, artists, industrialists, and others whose deeds made American history have left their mark in this state. So, along with the go-kart tracks, miniature golf courses, and water slides, museums and historic sites appear with regularity on the list of attractions families will enjoy.

Arranged first by county and then alphabetically by town within each of the eight chapters, each destination includes basic information such as names, addresses, and telephone numbers, and a brief but detailed review of what families can expect to see (or learn or explore) at that location. Hours and fees are provided, but remember that these are subject to change. Always call ahead to make sure that you are not surprised by a new policy.

If you have special needs such as handicapped access or changing facilities, call before you depart. Families with infants and toddlers may also benefit from an inquiry about the use of strollers, knapsacks, child carriers, and so on. Inquiries about the use of cameras and audio and video recorders may also spare you any disappointment. Remember, too, that exhibits and facilities change—even locations may shift, and unfortunately, some places close down altogether. Write to me in care of The Globe Pequot Press, at P.O. Box 833, Old Saybrook, Connecticut 06475, if you discover changes you'd like to pass along for future editions.

The maps at the beginning of each chapter are intended to provide a quick reference to the towns covered in each county. Not intended to replace a good highway map or to provide routes for driving tours, the maps nonetheless should help you gain a general sense of the area and help you plan your visits to the attractions described in the chapter. Indexes in the back of the book are arranged first alphabetically and then by category to help you find your interests quickly.

You may want to supplement this guide with the generally excellent materials provided by the State of Connecticut Department of Economic Development. An annually updated vacation guide is available by calling (800) CT–BOUND. That office also provides a bounty of materials on such tourist-related topics as campgrounds, state parks, pick-your-own farms, maple sugar houses, historical commissions, and much more. In addition, each region of Connecticut has its own tourist commission, and the folks in those offices are there to assist you.

Even a cursory look through the pages of this book will reveal an obvious emphasis on the state of Connecticut itself and on its varied attractions. Don't be deceived, however. Less obviously, the spirit of the book resides in the heart of its title—it is a celebration of family and a celebration of adventure within the context of that unit. How lucky you are that Connecticut is the tool you will use for insight into yourselves as a family. Not only will you learn much about science, nature, history, and other fun subjects as you travel the picturesque byways of this pretty New England state, but you will also learn much about each other.

Scientist and naturalist Rachel Carson wrote, "If a child is to keep alive his inborn sense of wonder, he needs the companionship of at least one adult who can share it, rediscovering with him the joy, excitement, and mystery of the world we live in." In that vein, I invite you to use this travel guide to your advantage. Urge each other toward new experiences. Challenge yourselves to explore what you have not yet discovered. Learn about a topic you have never been taught. Open your eyes to sights you have never before paused to consider. Most importantly, use this travel guide to nurture the curiosity, the playfulness, and the imagination of every member of your family. These are the gifts that will sustain you.

As you adventure, collect only memories, take only photographs, leave only footprints. Have a wonderful time.

The prices and rates listed in this guidebook were confirmed at press time. We recommend, however, that you call establishments to obtain current information before traveling.

FAIRFIELD COUNTY

Widely known as Connecticut's wealthiest, busiest, and most densely populated area, Fairfield County offers a distinctive mix of attractions that belies its stereotyped reputation. True, vast estates fight for space alongside sleek corporate headquarters and suburban enclaves, but more—much more—is also here along this coastal plain that provides the gateway to New England. Fast-paced urban centers, quiet country waysides, and sandy beaches are all part of the very eclectic collection of Fairfield County destinations families can enjoy.

BETHEL/WEST REDDING/REDDING/EASTON

The area between Danbury to the north and Fairfield to the south is sliced vertically in two by Route 58, a great road for taking you through some lovely countryside. Give yourselves a break and meander here awhile. Your first stop is for ice cream. What's more adventurous than taking a handful of children into an ice cream parlor and inviting them to choose from a score or more of flavors? We're not recommending any garden-variety chain-store flavors, either. We're stopping for what the doctor recommends—**Dr. Mike's Ice Cream,** that is, at 158 Greenwood Avenue in Bethel. If you love rich, creamy, coat-your-throat ice cream, you're going to love Dr. Mike's. What's that saying—"If Mama ain't happy, ain't nobody

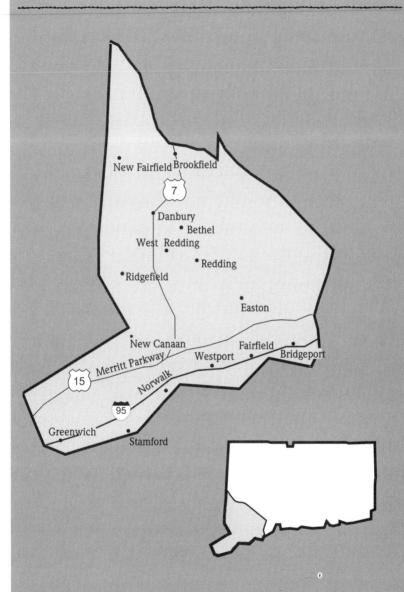

New Fairfield Brookfield

7

Danbury
Bethel
West Redding
Redding
Ridgefield
Easton
New Canaan
Fairfield
Merritt Parkway
Westport
Bridgeport
15
Norwalk
95
Greenwich
Stamford

Fairfield County

happy?" Well, after that chocolate ice cream, we-all sure was happy. Dr. Mike's is open from noon to 11:00 P.M. daily in the summer. Winter hours are shorter. Call 792–4388.

Actually, this whole area is delicious. Farms and produce stands, cider mills, and syrup sheds are liberally sprinkled throughout these parts. **Blue Jay Orchards** at 125 Plumtrees Road in Bethel has a roadside market chockablock with good, better, and best New England farm foods. You can call them at 748–0119 for pick-your-own information. Special events include a Strawberry Festival in June, an Apple Festival in late September or so, hayrides to the pumpkin patch in October, and a Christmas tree sale in December. We've been here when the joint was jumping—arts and crafts, hayrides, storytellers, hundreds of red-cheeked kids having a ball. We've also been here when the joint was sleepy as a dog in August—a few sad jars of honey, some overripe tomatoes, and the only thing moving was the dust on the road. You might like it better one way or the other—we like it both ways just fine.

If you'd like to visit other farms in the area, try some of these:

❋ **Warrups Farm,** 51 John Read Road, West Redding. Call 938–9403. Vegetables, pumpkins, maple syrup (demonstrations 10:00 A.M. to 5:00 P.M. during the first three weekends in March), beautiful country lane, free-range poultry, barnyard animals, and more.

❋ **Silverman's,** 451 Sport Hill Road (Route 59) Easton. Call 261–3306. Apples, pumpkins, pears, peaches, cider mill, market, barnyard.

❋ **Maple Row Tree Farm,** 538 North Park Avenue, Easton. Call 262–9577. Christmas trees, wreaths, horse-drawn wagon rides, hot cider. Open weekends from Thanksgiving to Christmas.

Going south on Route 58, you'll find **Putnam Memorial State Park** between Bethel and Redding at the junction near Route 107. Site of the 1778–79 winter encampment of General Israel Putnam's Northern Brigades of the Continental Army, the park includes a Revolutionary War museum built upon the original picket post from which the sentries guarded the barracks and magazine. It is open from Memorial Day to Columbus Day from 11:00 A.M. to 5:00 P.M. daily.

You can see the remains of the soldier's huts and the gunpowder magazine, a reconstruction of the officers' barracks, and a guardhouse reproduction. A bronze statue of "Old Put" shaking his fist at the British from
atop his trusty steed stands at the entrance to the park. Reenactments of
the Revolutionary War encampment, complete with artillery demonstrations and cavalry and infantry camp-life activities, are presented during the
annual Patriots' Weekend, usually in July. Call 938–2285.

The park is open year-round from 8:00 A.M. to dusk. Fishing, hiking,
and picnicking attract summer visitors; winter brings cross-country skiers.

BRIDGEPORT

If you decide to forgo a visit to Bridgeport because of the tarnished reputation of this once-thriving city, you will miss a wealth of activities perfect-
ly suited to children. Begin your tour at the north end of the city at the
Discovery Museum at 4550 Park Avenue (Merritt Parkway, exit 47).
Hands-on in nearly every way, this museum contains interactive exhibits
in the areas of art, science, and a smattering of industry, all specially
designed for children ages three to twelve.

The first floor's Interactive Art Gallery teaches kids about color, line,
and perspective—"paint" with a computer, then print out your creation,
spin the color wheels to "mix" new colors, shift stained "glass" puzzle
pieces to create mood changes, or duck into Walk into Color, a cave-like
structure that plays red, blue, and yellow music.

Upstairs, learn about nuclear energy, electronics, electricity, magnet-
ism, and light. Take a simulated bumper car ride to test your reaction time;
hear Alexander Graham Bell's first telephone transmission; use your body
to create a swirling wall of color in the Light Gallery.

The bottom floor includes a learning space with simplified hands-on
science and art for the youngest visitors. This floor is also home to the
Henry B. DuPont III Planetarium. Daily shows offer a dramatic look at
the heavens; programs change seasonally. The museum is the site of one
of the nation's sixteen **Challenger Learning Centers,** a computer-simu-
lated mission control and space station where participants perform experiments and collect data as astronauts would. Mini-missions are offered to
the public on weekends; call for reservations.

Special children's programs, workshops, and camps are offered throughout the year. Open year-round Tuesday to Saturday 10:00 A.M. to 5:00 P.M., and Sunday noon to 5:00 P.M. and, in July and August, on Mondays 10:00 A.M. to 5:00 P.M. The museum is closed on major holidays. Admission is $6.00 for adults, $4.00 for children ages four to eighteen. Call 372–3521 for information.

Beardsley Zoological Gardens (1875 Noble Avenue) ought to be on every family's list of places to go in Connecticut. Currently undergoing a major renovation, the facility has many new exhibits throughout its thirty-three-acre site inside the 130-acre Beardsley Park. Rare or endangered species such as Siberian tigers, red wolves, and sandhill cranes live here, as do 120 other species.

A New England farmyard features a cow, goats, geese, and sheep. Our favorite is the red-headed pig. The New World Tropics building is an outstanding South American rainforest re-creation. Toucans, woolly monkeys, tortoises, ocelots, and marmosets live in this excellent exhibit. A greenhouse with rare and tropical plants, a gift shop, snack bar, and picnic grove are on the grounds. In addition, an area is being prepared for the reinstallation of Bridgeport's famed Pleasure Beach Carousel.

The zoo is open from 9:00 A.M. to 4:00 P.M. daily, except Thanksgiving, Christmas, and New Year's Day. Admission to the zoo is $4.00 per adult, $2.00 per child, and children under three are free. Beardsley Park requires an additional parking fee of $3.00 for Connecticut vehicles and $5.00 for out-of-state vehicles. For information, call 576–8082.

To get to the next three Bridgeport attractions, take Route 8/25 South to exit 3 and follow the ramp to Main Street South.

On your way south on Main Street, you'll notice signs on your right for the **Downtown Cabaret Theater** (263 Golden Hill Street) and on your left for the **Port Jefferson Ferry.** To reach the theater, takie a right onto Golden Hill Street, at the third light after you've left exit 3. Once on Golden Hill, look for the theater's banner at the top of the hill.

Every weekend, the theater stages professional, award-winning productions from Broadway hits to musical reviews. Matinee and evening performances are given cabaret-style; patrons sit at round tables and bring their own picnics and refreshments. Productions for children are offered weekends from May through October. Tickets are about $7.00; subscriptions to all six shows each season are $36.00. For birthday parties, the whole company sings "Happy Birthday" to the feted child!

Security parking is available in the City Hall lot across from the theater. You can park on the street, but at your own risk—some folks around here collect radios, if you know what I mean. Call 576–1636.

Continue south on Main Street until you see signs for **The Bridgeport to Port Jefferson Steamboat Company** to your left. It operates a year-round ferry service that is more excursion boat than commuter transportation, but you can use it to get by car to the prettier parts of Long Island more quickly than you'd go via New York City or the Throgs Neck bridge. You can travel on the ferry on foot, with bicycles, or with your car to Port Jefferson, a small village of shops and restaurants that cater to daytrippers. Sailing time on the ferry is about an hour and a half each way. For schedules and rates, call 367–3043.

If you would rather tour a museum than take a boat ride or see a show, go straight through downtown until you reach 820 Main Street, the address of the sandstone delight formerly known as the Barnum Institute of Science and Industry and now just simply as the **Barnum Museum.** As you pass through its doors, prepare to enter the "Greatest Show on Earth" and one of the best museums between New York and Boston. Dedicated to the life and times of Phineas Taylor (P.T.) Barnum and his incredible impact on the world, the museum also celebrates the remarkable industrial heritage of Bridgeport and the culture of the circus in general. The first floor concentrates on Barnum the showman, entrepreneur, politician, and journalist. You'll be drawn into his magic from the minute you step inside this must-see museum.

A real (stuffed) elephant in the lobby sets the tone, and it only gets better from there. Make sure the kids watch the excellent short clip from the movie *Barnum* so they get a fix on who Barnum was.

On the second floor, you'll get a sense of the once-great city of Bridgeport in its heyday. A fabulous exhibit of all the products invented here will surprise those who only know Bridgeport from the tragic reports of its decay and near-demise on the nightly news.

On the third floor (our girls' hands-down favorite), enter the circus. See Barnum's Fejee Mermaid, the two-headed calf, a real Egyptian mummy, Tom Thumb and Lavinia Warren's clothing and furniture, and the incredible Brinley's circus, a hand-carved five-ring extravaganza, constructed completely to scale and massive even in miniature.

Downstairs again, a changing exhibition gallery, one of the largest such spaces in New England, offers traveling shows of interest to the whole family. Model trains, carousel animals, circus posters, and the original artwork from *Babar the Elephant* have been among recent exhibitions.

Museum hours are 10:00 A.M. to 4:30 P.M. Tuesday through Saturday and noon to 4:30 P.M. on Sunday. Admission is $5.00 for adults and $3.00 for children ages four to eighteen. For information, call 331–3304.

Next on a Bridgeport tour should be **Captain's Cove Seaport** (One Bostwick Avenue), home of the H.M.S. *Rose,* a fully-rigged British frigate and the only example of a Revolutionary War-era warship afloat today. The world's largest operational wooden vessel, the beautifully restored *Rose* is often used as a training ship or as a goodwill ambassador to other ports. When she's home, you can tour her; adults pay $3.00; children under twelve pay $2.00.

The Seaport itself, on historic Black Rock Harbor, includes a 500–seat restaurant, a fish market, and a charming boardwalk filled with craft shops, boutiques, and galleries. No admission is charged to stroll, shop, or watch the boats in the marina. Concerts, festivals, and other events are planned daily. Call 335–1433.

Bridgeport's other live theater—in fact, its oldest continuously running theater—overlooks Long Island Sound on Pleasure Beach Island. Called by the *New York Times* "the quintessential community theatre," **The Polka Dot Playhouse** presents four productions from late June through October. Anyone interested is welcome to audition. A summer theater workshop for children results in a children's production in late July and early August. Though perhaps to be moved if Donald Trump brings his money to Bridgeport to build a casino, the Polka Dot is still out on the Island as it has been for forty years. Take exit 29 off I–95 and follow the signs *directly* to Seaview Avenue. For information, call 333–3666.

BROOKFIELD

Brookfield town center is hardly more than a smile wide, and the Brookfield countryside is so pretty you may miss the center altogether. Before you drive straight through, though, stop at two of its best features. The **Brookfield Craft Center** on Route 25 right near its junction with Route 7 is a nationally known school for fine crafts with a multitude of classes in many media for children and adults. Open daily year-round except on major holidays, visitors can take one-hour tours of the workshops, gallery, and book and gift shop housed in nineteenth-century buildings overlooking Halfway Falls at a picturesque turn in the road. Those interested in classes can pick up the center's brochure or call ahead and ask them to mail one. Recent offerings for its summer youth program have included papermaking, bead weaving, drawing and painting, Native American pottery, and outdoor sculptures, among others. Adult programs have included jewelry making, boatbuilding, weaving, basketry, pottery, and more. Tours are given Monday through Saturday, 10:00 A.M. to 5:00 P.M., and Sunday from noon to 5:00 P.M. Call 775–4526 for information.

A few restaurants and a handful of shops make Brookfield a nice place to spend an afternoon. One of those shops is the second of Brookfield's best two downtown features. **Mother Earth Gallery and Mining Company** (806 Federal Road, which is Route 7) looks like an ordinary storefront with a neat inventory—crystals, minerals, shells, candles, and other environmentally friendly merchandise. It's also something more.

It has a simulated mine in it full of crystals and minerals and semiprecious stones. Kids can go prospecting in it with a bucket and miner's hard hat complete with headlamp. Plan your birthday party here for $16.50 per guest or go prospecting for $10 per person any time during regular store hours. Ask for their listing of places to really go prospecting in Connecticut. There are gems still left in these hills, and Mother Earth sells the equipment you'll need to find them. Open Wednesday through Saturday from 10:00 A.M. to 6:00 P.M., Sunday from noon to 5:00 P.M., and Monday from 10:00 A.M. to 6:00 P.M. Call 775–6272.

DANBURY

A small city famous for its 200-year history of hat manufacturing, Danbury was once also known for its incredible state fair, for many years the largest of Connecticut's agricultural fairs. This extravaganza of blue-ribbon pies, pigs, and pony pulls no longer exists, but in its memory Danbury is now home to one of Connecticut's largest malls, aptly named **Danbury Fair.** Nowhere else in this book will I recommend a mall, but this one is special for one reason. It has a double-decker carousel in its food court. Manufactured in Italy, this full-sized fiberglass wonder has mirrors, jewels, flowers, murals, and gallant steeds galore. Plus, as my kids say, "an upstairs." They charged 50 cents a ride last time we were there, all or part of which is donated to children's charities. The mall is at the junction of Route 7 and I–84. You can reach it from Route 7 or exit 3 on I–84. Park near the food court sign and follow the music.

Danbury is also the site of the beautiful **Charles Ives Center for the Arts** (Mill Plain Road, Westside Campus, Route 6). Spread over thirty-nine acres of lawn and woods, the center offers top-drawer entertainment in an open-air gazebo-covered stage throughout the summer months. Named for the Pulitzer prize–winning composer considered the father of American music, the center invites symphonies, jazz, folk, blues, theater, dance, and popular artists to its summer stage.

"Sunday in the Park" performances, perhaps four or five each season, are perfect for families, who are encouraged to bring blankets and picnics. Free admission is the policy for these 2:00 P.M. performances. Hiking trails, a picnic grove, and a variety of seasonal fairs and festivals are all part of the fun here. For information, call 837–9226.

Danbury has other attractions families might enjoy. For space reasons alone, two are listed here with only a brief description: The **Scott–Fanton Museum** at 43 Main Street includes the 1785 John Rider House, the John Doff Shop with hat industry exhibits, the Charles Ives birthplace, a Revolutionary War exhibit, and a woodworking display. Call 743–5200.

Tarrywile Park at 70 Southern Boulevard features trails, ponds, and historic buildings, including Tarrywile Mansion and Hearthstone Castle (not currently open to the public). You can hike, cross-country ski, ice-skate, sled, picnic, horseback ride, and camp here. Call 744–3130.

FAIRFIELD

As one of Connecticut's oldest towns, it's not surprising that Fairfield offers an excellent historical site for those interested in pre–Revolutionary War life. Owned and operated by the Fairfield Historical Society, **Ogden House and Gardens** (1520 Bronson Road) is a meticulously researched and restored 1750 saltbox farmhouse furnished to portray the lives of its first inhabitants, Jane and David Ogden. An eighteenth-century kitchen garden and a native wildflower woodland garden are also on the picturesque property.

A Hands-On History Camp for children ages eight to eleven is held annually during the second week in July. The program offers cooking, tin lantern piercing, taffy pulling, eighteenth-century games, and more. Birthday parties at the house consist of a tour with a costumed docent portraying Mrs. Ogden, hoop rolling lessons, and crafts such as candle dipping, wood carving, or corn-husk doll making. An ongoing schedule of workshops for children has recently included teddy bear repair, tombstone study, and principles of archaeology with a simulated dig. Public tours are given from mid-May through mid-October on Saturdays and Sundays only from 1:00 to 4:00 P.M. Admission is $2.00 for adults; $1.00 for children twelve and under. For information, call 259–1598.

If you think Ogden House is for the birds, you're wrong. It's the Connecticut Audubon Society's **Birdcraft Museum and Sanctuary** that is for the birds—and it's a great place for families, too. Just a spit south of I–95 at 314 Unquowa Road, this tiny six-acre enclave was founded in 1914 as the first songbird sanctuary in the United States. Documented records of more than 120 species of birds have been kept for this vest-pocket site. Huge maples hung with vines, century-old rhododendrons, sassafras, and highbush cranberry are along the trail through the woods and across a wooden boardwalk above a shallow pond. Sit awhile in the gazebo and listen to the birds and frogs. Look for the nesting night herons.

Inside the turn-of-the-century museum, browse through galleries featuring the birds and mammals of New England, grouped in dioramas by habitat and by seasons. The murals are exceptional. A gallery of African animals, a changing exhibit gallery, and a book and gift shop complete the facility.

The Birdcraft is not a hands-on extravaganza. Still, it offers opportunities for children to touch, listen, and observe. This little gem of a museum and the sanctuary are open year-round on Tuesday, Saturday, and Sunday from 9:00 A.M. to 5:00 P.M. Admission is $2.00 for adults; children under fourteen are $1.00. Call 259–0416.

In the north end of town is one of my favorite spots, just a bicycle ride from my childhood home. A "graduate" of several of the many courses offered here for children, I know this place well indeed. The spot is the **Roy and Margot Larsen Bird Sanctuary** and the Connecticut Audubon Society's **Fairfield Nature Center** (2325 Burr Street). Created on reclaimed farm property, this beautiful tract of New England woodland was built as a model wildlife sanctuary juxtaposing habitats and trails to allow people to experience the diversity without disturbing the refuge. Marsh, ponds, streams, meadows, coniferous forest, and second-growth areas of hardwoods are among the Sanctuary's habitats. Its six miles of trails include a Walk for the Disabled.

The Nature Center includes natural science exhibits, live animal displays, a gift shop/bookstore and the Educational Animal Compound of nonreleasable animals the Connecticut Audubon Society has rehabilitated.

Summer camps, guided walks, junior naturalist programs, and field trips are numerous. The Nature Center is open year-round, Tuesday through Saturday, from 9:00 A.M. to 4:30 P.M.; closed on major holidays. The Sanctuary is open daily, year-round, from dawn to dusk. Children under twelve are admitted free; adults are charged $2.00. Call 259–6305.

By the way, this area of town known as Greenfield Hill is heavily planted with dogwoods and is famed for its annual **Dogwood Festival** in mid-May. A great outing for Mother's Day or any other reason, it provides one of the best opportunities I know to enjoy the beauty of springtime in Connecticut. For information, call the Fairfield Town Hall.

Before you leave Fairfield, go back down Burr Street and straight down Mill Plain Road all the way to the Post Road (Route 1). Take a left onto the Post Road and a right a few blocks down onto Reef Road and stop at **Timothy's Ice Cream.** Geoff, ice-cream man extraordinaire, has invented many of Timothy's original flavors, which keep the line going out the door all summer long. Try the Black Rock ice cream—trust me. Hours vary seasonally. For information, call 255–5188.

GREENWICH

Visitors approaching Fairfield County from the New York border on I–95 or the Merritt Parkway won't have far to drive for a full day of family-perfect activities. Start your day in Greenwich at the **Bruce Museum** (1 Museum Drive; follow signs from I–95 exit 3). Once a dark dinosaur of a natural history museum with an impressive but largely stored collection of art and artifacts, it has undergone a magnificent multimillion-dollar expansion and renovation. Now one of the most sophisticated and state-of-the-art museums in the region, the Bruce was doubled in size around the 1853 mansion conveyed to the Town of Greenwich in 1908 by textile merchant Robert Moffatt Bruce.

Today, it houses 25,000 objects in three categories: fine and decorative arts, cultural history, and environmental sciences. Pre-Columbian and Native American artifacts; nineteenth-century American paintings, prints, and sculpture; costumes, pottery, and more are in the art galleries. Changing exhibitions feature such diverse collections as textiles, dollhouses, and mechanical banks

The environmental science galleries focus on the past 500 years of local New England history and ecology, taking visitors from ancient to modern times via an environmental perspective. Within this wing, the cave-like minerals gallery preserves a collection of ores, crystals, precious stones, and fluorescent minerals. An archaeological dig depicts the discovery of the Manakaway site on Greenwich Point and includes artifacts unearthed during the excavation. Interactive exhibits allow visitors to experience the evolution and ecology of Long Island Sound. The environmental galleries also include a simulated wigwam of the Eastern Woodland Indians, a cross-section of a tidal marsh ecosystem, a marine touch tank, a diorama that takes audiences from dawn to dusk in a coastal woodland ecosystem, an Ecological Awareness gallery focusing on tree and water communities, and an interactive wall narrating the history of Long Island Sound.

The Bruce offers a continuous schedule of festivals, workshops, concerts, and educational programs. Trust me. This is a museum families will love. The museum is open Tuesday through Saturday, 10:00 A.M. to 5:00 P.M.; Sunday, 2:00 to 5:00 P.M. Closed Monday and major holidays. Adult admission is $3.50; children ages five to twelve pay $2.50; under-fives are free. No admission is charged on Tuesday. Call 869–0376.

The **Bruce Memorial Park and Playground** immediately adjacent to the museum is a great place to rest, run, or picnic while you are here. Views of a real tidal marsh and Long Island Sound provide the backdrop. Look for the herons that inhabit the area—they are beautiful.

In the northern reaches of Greenwich is the beautiful **Audubon Center** (613 Riversville Road at the corner of John Street). Eight miles of trails lead through 280 acres of woodlands, meadows, ponds, and streams. The Interpretive Building houses an art gallery, a demonstration beehive, a bird observation window, a backyard wildlife habitat, and the excellent Environmental Book and Gift Shop. Loop trail options are available to fit schedules and hiking abilities. The Discovery Trail leads past a great little pond replete in summer with bullfrogs, duckweed, and dragonflies. Stay on the trail long enough and you'll walk right across the top of a lovely waterfall at the edge of Mead Lake. The landscape here is extraordinarily pretty and restful. The trees, both those standing and fallen, are among the most awesome specimens we have seen in Connecticut.

The Audubon Center offers a large variety of outdoor walks, camps, and naturalist workshops for children, adults, and environmental science teachers. General admission to the center's trails and the Interpretive Building is $3.00 for adults and $1.50 for children.

Visitors can also walk the trails of a second parcel just a mile away on North Porchuck Road. There, the 127-acre **Fairchild Connecticut Wildflower Garden** offers 8 miles of trails through native flowering plants and ferns. Established as an example of naturalistic landscaping, the garden is especially inviting in the spring. Both parcels are open year-round. The Fairchild Garden is open daily from dawn to dusk. The Audubon Center is open Tuesday through Sunday from 9:00 A.M. to 5:00 P.M. It is closed on Mondays and holiday weekends. For information, call 869–5272.

If pre-Revolutionary War history, architecture, and lifestyles interest you, don't leave Greenwich until you've visited the Bush–Holley House and Putnam Cottage. The 1732 **Bush–Holley House** (39 Strickland Road in the Cos Cob section) is a classic central-chimney saltbox. Once the home of farmer and mill owner David Bush and later a boardinghouse operated by the Holley family, the house is the site of one of the first American Impressionist art colonies. Impressionist artists, including Childe Hassam and J. Alden Weir, painted here during the period from 1890 to 1925. A collection of their works and an artist's studio complete with easels, paints, brushes, and more are on display, along with a fine collection of household implements, tools, furniture, and textiles. Children may attend History Week annually during July to learn, hands-on, about eighteenth-century hearth cooking, needlework, sheep shearing, and other activities. At Christmastime (call for schedule) the house is decorated in a Victorian theme for candlelight tours. The house is open for tours from February through December, Tuesday to Friday, noon to 4:00 P.M.; Sunday, 1:00 to 4:00 P.M. Adult admission is $4.00; students twelve and over are $3.00; children under twelve are free. Call 869–6899.

Putnam Cottage (243 East Putnam Avenue, which is Route 1), built circa 1692, was formerly known as Knapp Tavern and was used during the Revolution as a meeting place for military leaders, including former resident Israel Putnam, second in command to George Washington during the War. Restored to appear as it might have in 1700, its fish-scale shingles, fieldstone fireplaces, and eighteenth-century herb garden are among its special features. Its collection includes Putnam's desk, Bible, glasses, the mirror through which he supposedly saw the British coming, and the uniform he wore during the War (one of seven Revolutionary War uniforms known to exist). The Daughters of the American Revolution offers tours from April through January on Wednesday, Friday, and Saturday from 1:00 to 4:00 P.M. Adults are $2.00; under-twelves are free. Call 869–9697.

NEW CANAAN

Exquisite in nearly every way is the gracious and affluent suburb of New Canaan, just north of Stamford via Routes 137 or 106. Its village center is chock-ful of boutiques, restaurants, bakeries, and bookstores (such as the excellent **New Canaan Book Shop** on Elm Street), many suited to or designed for fulfilling the whims of children. Before you're overdrawn, put away the checkbook and stop at two of Fairfield County's treasures: the New Canaan Nature Center and the New Canaan Historical Society. The first is a true respite from the thrust and parry of Fairfield County's version of civilization. Located on forty acres of diverse habitats, the **New Canaan Nature Center** (144 Oenoke Ridge) includes 2 miles of trails and board-walk through meadow, woods, and marsh and past two ponds.

A bird-watching platform, a wildflower garden, a butterfly field, a maple syrup shed, an orchard, a cider house, and an herb garden are all on the property. The excellent Discovery Center houses hands-on exhibits in the natural sciences, some particularly well suited to young children. See a living bee colony, crawl through a "burrow," make leaf rubbings, build a bug with giant Velcro-backed plastic body parts, handle animal homes and hides, make animal tracks with rubber stamps and ink, and more. Learn about soil, seeds, mineral fluorescence, geological formations, migration, and animal defense mechanisms. Check out the snakes, newts, turtles, and fish in several habitat tanks, and stop by the exceptional gift shop.

Back outside is the Wildlife Rehabilitation area, home to a broad-winged hawk and a great horned owl. Next door is the solar greenhouse—rest at the edge of its goldfish pond, which has a really neat fountain in it. The Nature Center offers a fantastic schedule of lectures, walks, day camps, live animal demonstrations, and excursions like canoeing, hiking, and bicycle trips. It also offers natural science birthday parties, early childhood parent/child programs, and annual special events.

The Discovery Center is open year-round, Tuesday through Saturday from 9:30 A.M. to 4:30 P.M. and on Sundays from 12:30 to 4:30 P.M. The trails and grounds are open daily from dawn to dusk. Donations are accepted; family memberships are encouraged. Call 966–9577.

At 13 Oenoke Ridge is the **New Canaan Historical Society.** "Blech—let's skip it," your kids might say. Not so fast. This one has five separate buildings housing seven museums and a library. The 1764 Hanford–Silliman House is furnished in the style of its eighteenth- and nineteenth-century inhabitants and includes collections of dolls, toys, and quilts. The Tool Museum houses tools of the housewright, cabinetmaker, wheelwright, wainwright, tanner, farmer, cooper, farrier, and shoemaker, all arranged for a clear understanding of their use. The fully operational New Canaan Hand Press is a re-creation of a nineteenth-century printing office built around a rare Smith-Hoe Acorn iron press. The 1878 John Rogers Studio and Museum, dedicated to the work of the famed "people's sculptor" of the same name, houses a collection of Roger's work actually sculpted in the studio. The 1799 Rock School is an orginal New Canaan one-room schoolhouse, with benches, desks, wood stove, and more to complete the ambience of an early nineteenth-century classroom.

Inside the Town House, which also houses the society's library and special exhibition room, are the Costume Museum and Cody Drug Store. The Costume Museum is outstanding and extensive. Changing exhibitions span the 200 years of American life the collection represents. Settings are built on such themes as Roaring Twenties, Gay Nineties, or Women of Leisure. Cody Drug Store contains most of the actual interior of the 1845 original store, once located on New Canaan's Main Street. All fixtures, bottles, scrip books, patent medicines, and even the ice-cream parlor are from the original store.

Call ahead if you would like a family tour of all the buildings. The Town House is open year-round, Tuesday through Saturday from 9:30 A.M. to 12:30 P.M. and from 2:00 P.M. to 4:30 P.M. The other buildings are open during July and August on Tuesday, Wednesday, Thursday, Friday, and Sunday from 2:00 to 4:00 P.M., and from September through June on Wednesday, Thursday, and Sunday from 2:00 to 4:00 P.M. Admission is free. Call 966–1776.

NEW FAIRFIELD

North of Danbury, about as far north as you can go in Fairfield County, are two popular recreational destinations: Candlewood Lake and Squantz Pond State Park. While **Candlewood Lake** is considerably larger, public access is limited. The largest artificial lake in Connecticut, it was built in 1925 to provide hydroelectric power to the region and is now bordered by private residences. Public boat launches are available at some of the town beaches on the perimeter, and there are docks at two restaurants on the east shore (Down the Hatch and the Candlewood Inn). Sadly enough, though it's pretty as a picture and you can drive to the lakeside from many side streets, residents will challenge you if you take a dip from their waterfront. The best bet for swimming here is **Squantz Pond State Park.**

This pretty area of hills and woodlands surrounds Squantz Pond, a small arm of Candlewood Lake. The park offers a boat launch from which boaters can gain access to Candlewood. Summer fun here includes waterskiing, fishing, swimming, scuba diving, and picnicking. In winter, use the park for ice-skating and cross-country skiing. A food concession and canoe rentals are available in summer. Call 797–4165.

NORWALK

Norwalk used to be a small city with a big bad reputation, and as with lots of bad reputations, some criticism was fair and some was not. True, this once-proud port suffered inner-city decay and accompanying crime statistics that sent tourists scurrying, but that's a fact of the past. Downtown and on down to the docks is a thoroughly revitalized area that does the city's forefathers proud.

Start your tour of Norwalk at the **Maritime Center,** the flagship, if you will, of the bustling, artsy SoNo (South Norwalk) neighborhood. At 10 North Water Street near the corner of Washington Street, this aquarium-cum-theater-cum-maritime museum is a celebration of life near, on, and under the sea, particularly Long Island Sound. Located in a restored nineteenth-century foundry overlooking Norwalk Harbor, this major attraction includes twenty-two aquariums filled with 125 species of marine life.

Interactive and video displays throughout the aquarium tell the secrets of the fragile ecosystems of Long Island Sound. Visitors move from one marine habitat re-creation to another, beginning at the salt marsh and culminating at a 110,000-gallon tank with sharks, stingrays, bluefish, and other creatures of the open ocean. Changing exhibitions feature other topics related to the sea.

Handle sea stars, crabs, and other tidal pool inhabitants in the touch tank. Learn about water and wave movement in the Waterworks exhibit. Watch craftspeople build boats in the centuries-old tradition of New England boat builders. Discover the uses of boats such as the dory, sandbagger, and sharpie as you learn about marine navigation and Norwalk's oyster industry.

Before you go home, watch an IMAX film in the six-story-high theater. You might experience the secrets of the *Titanic,* the rainforest, or a beaver lodge, in whatever film is scheduled. An eight-story-wide screen and Sensaround sound system keep you on the edge of your seat.

Special events, camps, and workshops are commonplace at the Maritime Center. Each is wonderfully tailored to children of specific or all ages. An excellent gift shop and an oyster bar and snack bar are also on site. The Maritime Center should be on everyone's list of places to go in Connecticut.

The Maritime Center is open daily year-round, except Thanksgiving, Christmas, and New Year's Day. Regular hours are 10:00 A.M. to 5:00 p.m.; from Memorial Day to Labor Day, it stays open until 6:00 P.M. The IMAX theater runs during center hours and is also open for Friday and Saturday evening shows. Admission is charged to the center alone, to the IMAX alone, or to both together. Adults are $7.50, $5.50, or $11.50, respectively. Children ages two to twelve are $6.50, $4.50, or $9.50; children under

Every member of the family can pick up crabs, whelk, egg cases, and other shoreline objects at the Maritime Center's Aquarium Touch Tank. (Photo by Bud Trenks/courtesy Maritime Center)

two are free. Parking is available at adjacent municipal lots at an additional cost. For information, call 852–0700.

One of our best summer excursions was a cruise on the ferryboat *Island Girl* to Sheffield Island, the outermost of the Norwalk Islands. From Hope Dock (just outside the south doors of the Maritime Center at the corner of Washington and Water streets), this clean and comfortable sixty-passenger vessel offers a thirty-minute cruise to the island, where one can disembark for an hour, or a whole day of beachcombing, bird-watching, picnicking, hiking, or touring the beautiful 1868 stone lighthouse.

The *Island Girl* crew and captain offer a lively narration on the trip to the island. Stories about the Washington Street drawbridge and Norwalk Harbor are mixed with explanations of the significance of buoys, folklore and legends of the islands themselves, and a smattering of references to the shore and seabirds of the area. Once at the island, passengers are free to spend their time as they choose. Most folks take the fifteen- to twenty-minute tour of the lighthouse. Several of its rooms, including bedrooms, dining room, and living room, are open to the public. Four flights of wooden stairs lead to the lovely black-capped light tower. (Decommissioned in 1902 when a new light was built a quarter-mile inshore, the lighthouse's original light is no longer in the tower.) If you have time, bring a picnic and spread a blanket under the tall oaks in the three-acre picnic grove for a leisurely brunch or lunch. No concessions are on the island, so bring snacks. Wear bathing suits and sunscreen so you can swim or comb the beach. Outhouses are provided.

The sixty-acre island also includes the **Stewart B. McKinney National Wildlife Refuge.** No trails are within its boundaries, but you can encircle the refuge by walking the perimeter of the island. Note the time if you set out on such an excursion. The last cruise departs the island at 3:00 P.M. on weekdays and 4:30 P.M. on weekends and holidays.

The island is also open to private boaters. A dinghy service transports sailors from moorings to the island dock at a charge of $4.00 per adult on the boat. *Island Girl* cruises sail weekends and holidays only from Memorial Day until the third week of June, leaving Hope Dock at 10:00 A.M., noon, and 2:00 P.M. From late June through Labor Day, cruises depart at 9:30 A.M. and 1:30 P.M. on weekdays, and on weekends and holidays at

9:30 A.M., 11:30 A.M., 1:30 P.M., and 3:30 P.M. Seating is first-come/first served. Arrive early to allow time for parking in the nearby lots. Adult tickets are $9.00; children under twelve are $7.00. For updated information, call the Norwalk Seaport Association at 838–9444. For special charters, call 334–9166.

When you disembark, stroll the SoNo district. Centered on Washington, Water, and South Main streets, SoNo is a neighborhood of boutiques, antiques shops, restaurants, and art galleries. Families might want to stop by **Molly Brody,** a dollhouse and miniatures store, **Beadworks,** a treasure chest of jewelry-making supplies, and **Toon Inn,** which sells original cels from animated films. Feel free to browse if you can't buy.

If you want to dine in SoNo, pick a place, any place. Since this book is an adventure guide, we're recommending you pick up a bite to eat at **Stew Leonard's** (100 Westport Avenue, which is Route 1) just so you can visit this most extravagant dairy store/bakery/supermarket perhaps anywhere (except, I guess, at the second Stew Leonard's in Danbury). Baked goods, dairy product, seafood and meats, produce, cut flowers, and a hot and cold buffet of lunch and dinner foods are not the main attraction here, though all are excellent and most are competitively priced. We're sending you here for the rock 'n' roll dairy band, the strolling 6-foot cows, the guitar-and-banjo-strumming horse and dog who croon toe-tapping tunes from velvet-draped stages, the talking cow at the milk conveyor belt, the egg-laying hen at the egg bin, the choir of singing lettuces and eggplants, and the barnyard animals in the mini-farm out front. If the crowds of shoppers don't slow you down, this amazing cast of characters will. You may have to drag children under ten out of here—you can entice them to exit by buying the soft-serve ice cream or yogurt they sell outside the main entrance. Watch kids *carefully* in the congested parking lot. Stew Leonard's is open daily year-round from 7:00 A.M. to 11:00 P.M. Call 847–7213.

Next in Norwalk is the **Lockwood–Mathews Mansion Museum** (295 West Avenue), just a hair north of SoNo and I–95. A National Historic Landmark, the lavish Victorian stone mansion is true extravagance—forget what I just told you about Stew Leonard's. This remarkable four-story château redefines splendor and elegance. Originally built in 1864 as a summer home for Norwalk native Legrand Lockwood, Wall Street investment banker and railroad magnate, the mansion features the craftsmanship of the finest American and European artisans of the time. Incredibly fine inlaid woodwork, etched glass, marble floors and columns, frescoed walls, gold-leafed ceilings, crystal chandeliers, sweeping staircases, and fine decorative arts of all kinds are found throughout the fifty rooms that surround the mansion's magnificent skylit octagonal rotunda. A beautiful collection of music boxes and other mechanical music devices is displayed on the second floor.

Hour-long guided tours of the mostly restored first and second floors are preceded by a short film describing the painstaking ongoing restoration. Annual events include a Victorian Ice Cream Social in early summer and a crafts fair in mid-July. Other special exhibitions are held each year.

The mansion is open from February 1 to mid-December, Tuesday through Friday from 10:00 A.M. to 3:00 P.M. and Sunday from 1:00 to 4:00 P.M. It is closed on major holidays. The last tour is given an hour prior to closing. Adult admission is $5.00; students pay $3.00, and children under twelve are free. For information, call 838–1434.

You might want to visit Norwalk on one of its famed festival days. In particular, try the **Norwalk Oyster Festival,** held annually on the weekend after Labor Day. The waterfront festival celebrates Long Island Sound and the area's seafaring past. Events include an arts and crafts show, tall ship tours, an oyster shucking contest, and foods and hoopla typical of summer festivals. According to the Connecticut Tourism Industry, the Oyster Festival is the best annual event in the state. For information, call 838–9444.

Also attracting thousands of visitors is the **SoNo Arts Celebration,** held each summer for nearly twenty years. Hundreds of artists exhibit their work in a sidewalk show spanning several blocks. Live-music dance parties, an antique auto parade, storytelling, a silent film fest, and a puppet parade are all part of the midsummer festivities. New events are added each year, but a continuing favorite is the Kinetic Sculpture race in which artists vying for prizes move their weird and wonderful contraptions over a 1-mile course through SoNo streets, using any human-powered means they choose. Look for the Children's Area with entertainment and hands-on projects specially designed for young artists. Call 866–7916.

RIDGEFIELD

While Fairfield County's coastal cities and towns become quieter and more rural as you leave the busy Route 1/I–95 corridor, it's not until you're inland 10 miles or so that you really notice Fairfield County's split personality. From points north, it is downright bucolic.The pace slows. The air is clean. You might even forget you are in the state's most densely populated region.

Ridgefield is one such town, and on its outskirts (in fact, half in the town of Wilton) lies the nation's newest National Park Historic Site. The first national park in Connecticut and the only one in the country dedicated to a painter, **Weir Farm** (735 Nod Hill Road) is the former home of noted American Impressionist J. Alden Weir (1852–1919), one of the foremost painters of his time. His country summer retreat from New York City, Weir Farm is the subject of many of his paintings.

Currently fifty-seven acres, the secluded site includes Weir's farmhouses, studios, and barns, all among the rocky meadows and rolling woodlands of the Danbury Hills. Is it a "family adventure" place? Well, it doesn't whir or whistle and it won't get you wet, but if you need a place to relax, a place to lose the Gameboy in, please do come here.

Life tenancy of resident artists Doris and Sperry Andrews restricts the National Park Service's use of the property somewhat, but the Andrewses graciously allow the public to take tours of the studios Wednesday through Saturday. If you are lucky enough to receive a tour in which one of the Andrewses participates, you will have a memorable visit indeed. Their presence adds to the ambience of a true artist's retreat.

A video introduction to Weir Farm's history and importance is offered at the Burlington House Visitor Center and the bulk of the property is open daily for strolling and bird-watching. Artists both professional and amateur are welcome to bring easels, paints, et cetera, for sketching anywhere on the public portions of the property. The Weir Farm Historic Painting Sites Trail features twelve sites that have been identified as the original inspiration for works of art done at the farm. The self-guided trail is mostly easy walking through woods, fields, and gardens, and along old stone walls and fences.

Bring a picnic if you want to spend the day here. If you arrive without art supplies and your children are inspired to draw, ask at the visitor center for the loan of a sketchpad and crayons. You might also ask about art classes offered for children and adults throughout the year.

The farm is open daily from April through October from 8:30 A.M. to 5:00 P.M. and at the same hours, Monday through Saturday, from November through March. Studio tours are Wednesday through Saturday at 10:00 A.M. Admission is free. For information, call 834–1896.

A little less secluded but nonetheless surprising to find in a small New England town like Ridgefield is the sophisticated **Aldrich Museum of American Art** (258 Main Street, which is Route 35). Founded by Larry Aldrich, a truly innovative connoisseur of fine art, the museum focuses its attention on new talents and currents in art and culture.

Located in a historic building with a stunning contemporary addition, the Aldrich includes a works by John Chamberlain, Eva Hesse, Robert Indiana, Jasper Johns, Roy Lichtenstein, Fairfield Porter, Andy Warhol, and many others. My girls' favorite was James Grashow's *Walking Building.*

A beautiful sculpture garden with many notable pieces makes a great picnic area, but it is not a playground. Please don't climb on the sculptures. The museum offers a great variety of workshops for children. Printmaking, chair painting, self-portraiture, and sculpting were on the most recent schedule. The museum is open year-round, Tuesday through Sunday, from 1:00 to 5:00 P.M. Adult admission is $3.00; students are $2.00. For information, call 438–4519.

Distinctly different in character is Ridgefield's historic **Keeler Tavern** (132 Main Street), built about 1730 and long reputed as the most hospitable stop on the overland coach route between New York and Boston. The tavern was also a hub of community life in Ridgefield. A meetingplace for supporters of the Patriot cause in Revolutionary War days, it was fired upon by British troops during the Battle of Ridgefield. A cannonball fired that day remains embedded in the house.

The tavern's taproom is an especially cheerful reminder of the comforts the inn must have offered to weary travelers of the eighteenth century. Though modified several times in its history, the tavern's rooms are furnished according to the period closest to its early days. Visitors can also see the ladies' parlor, dining room, bedchambers, and kitchen. Woodenware, cooking implements, and other domestic utensils illustrate the colonial lifestyle.

Keeler Tavern is open for tours from February through December. Hours are Wednesday, Saturday, Sunday, Monday, and holidays from 1:00 to 4:00 P.M. The last tour begins at 3:20 P.M. Adult admission is $3.00; children under twelve are $1.00. Call 438–5485.

STAMFORD

The city of Stamford offers excellent opportunities for family adventure. Start at the **Whitney Museum of American Art** (One Champion Plaza, at Atlantic Street and Tresser Boulevard), the Connecticut branch of the museum of the same name in New York City. Funded by Champion International, the museum offers five changing exhibitions of American art each year.

Because of its small size, this museum is wonderful for introducing children to art, particularly the twentieth-century works that form the backbone of the Whitney's collection. The museum's calendar of special events includes musical and dance performances, storytellers, puppetry shows, story readings, arts and crafts workshops, and family tours. The museum's airy ambience adds to its approachable nature, and an afternoon spent here is an afternoon well spent.

The Whitney is open year-round Tuesday through Saturday from 11:00 A.M. to 5:00 P.M. Admission is free, as is the parking in the Champion garage on Tresser Boulevard. Call 358–7630.

For quality time that's pricier than a day at the museum but well worth the cost, call the **Stamford Center for the Arts** (downtown at 307 Atlantic Street) for a schedule of performances at the Rich Forum or the Palace Theater. From September through May or June, the Rich generally offers Broadway-quality theater productions; the Palace offers single-night or short-run performances of music, dance, comedy, and more, including subscription series such as ballet, folk, classical, and others.

Many performances are suitable for the family. Take advantage of group rates, matinee performances, or seats in the upper tiers. Productions specifically for children are planned each summer; this year, tickets were $6.00. Two performances, at 11:00 A.M. and 3:30 P.M., are given each Wednesday. The Palace, by the way, is a fully restored masterpiece with incredible acoustics. For reservations or information, call 325–4466 or 358–2305.

If the reserved pace of the theater or the Whitney leaves you and the kids with energy to burn, you might want to head to **The Varsity Club** (74 Largo Drive in Riverbend Industrial Park), a 34,000-square-foot indoor recreational amusement center. This place will be a hit with almost any kid.

The very young will love the soft play/exercise area with trolleys, tunnels, slides, and obstacles to challenge both body and imagination. Older kids may want to scale Mount Varsity, a rock-climbing wall suited to beginners and veterans, both of whom are harnessed and supervised. Miniature golf, a spinning teacups ride, a futuristic Laser Tag arena, high-speed bumper cars, and hi-ball basketball are fun for all ages.

Lots more is here—computer games, pinball, arcade games, Skee-ball, air hockey, sit-down racing games, and a Malt Shop for sandwiches and snacks. Tickets are sold at $1.00 each; books of twelve tickets are $10.00. Activities range in price from $2.00 to $5.00; video game tokens are 25 cents each. The Varsity Club is open Sunday through Thursday from 10:00 A.M. to 10:00 P.M. and on Friday and Saturday from 10:00 A.M. to 11:00 P.M. Call 359–2582.

Not far from the Varsity Club is **United House Wrecking** at 535 Hope Street. You wouldn't plan an all-day excursion to this place, but its merchandise and sheer size have combined to place it irrevocably on Stamford's list of attractions. Architectural salvage—doors, stained-glass windows, mantels, chandeliers—is the main attraction for renovators, but the fun only begins there. An ever-changing array of normal, truly whimsical, and downright weird stuff is also here—weathervanes, telescopes, lanterns, umbrella stands, wishing wells, jewelry, traffic lights, toys, china, books, gargoyles, mooseheads, a barbershop pole, jukeboxes, wagon wheels, subway straphangers—in short, everything under the sun including bells, whistles, and the kitchen sink. The kids might not even guess this place is a store at first, but when they figure it out, you can bet they'll want to buy something. Open Monday through Saturday from 9:30 A.M. to 5:30 P.M. and Sunday from noon to 5:00 P.M. Call 348–5371.

If the smell of the salt breeze draws you away from downtown toward the water, try to catch a ride on the 80-foot Soundwaters *Eagle,* a three-masted sharpie schooner that offers three-hour "eco-cruises." Led by a trained naturalist and marine biologist, the cruises focus on the ecology, history, culture, and future of Long Island Sound. Three cruises leave daily from the dock at 4 Yacht Haven West Marina, Washington Boulevard. For information and reservations, call 323–1978.

Inland a fair distance, **The Stamford Museum and Nature Center** has been one of our favorite places for many years. North of the Merritt Parkway at 39 Scofieldtown Road, this 118-acre park has a variety of features like no other nature center we have visited in the state.

Heckscher Farm on the premises is a working New England farm recreation that includes a 1750 barn on hillside pastureland typical of self-sufficient farms of yesteryear. A garden sowed with heirloom seeds yields a bountiful autumn harvest, and animals such as a cow, pigs, goats, chickens, geese, oxen, sheep, and even a pair of river otters inhabit the enclosure. In the midst of the farm is a country store and a gem of an exhibit dedicated to eighteenth- and nineteenth-century farm life and tools.

Three miles of trails, a 300-foot streamside boardwalk, and a pond habitat with picnic area complement the renovated Overbrook Natural Science Center, which houses reptiles, amphibians, and four aquatic tanks that simulate habitats of these creatures of the woodland and its streams. A projection microscope allows individuals or classes to view frog eggs, insects, or other natural materials on an overhead screen. Outside the center a beautiful brick walkway edges a garden of native plants and flowers.

On the hillside nearest the parking area is the Stamford Museum, with seven galleries of changing fine art, Americana, nature displays, and a permanent exhibit on Native American life and history. Small but beautiful dioramas are the highlight of the Native American gallery; it also includes a birchbark canoe, a huge bison head, and many artifacts from four major North American Indian groups. The museum also is home to a planetarium and an observatory, with the largest telescope west of the Mississippi.

The museum is currently converting a wooded one-acre site to one of the most unusual playgrounds anywhere. An 8-foot-high hollow log leading to a 3-foot-long hollow branch will open onto a sandpit where kids can dig for dinosaur bone replicas. A 6-foot-high hollow stump will feature copies of insect galleries and honeycombs. Two 7-foot-wide hawks' nests in which to climb, a large-scale chipmunk burrow in which to rest, and a

30-foot-long otters' slide on which, of course, to slide are among other planned features. A water environment area will include play possibilities such as dam construction or boat racing. A treehouse, a beaver lodge replica, and a rope spider's web will complete the scene.

The staff conduct numerous workshops, lectures, festivals, and summer camps. Summer folk concerts, an autumn Harvest Fair, an Astronomy Day, and events such as maple sugaring, ice harvesting, and apple cidering are all on the Center's calender.

The Nature Center and Museum are open year-round, Monday through Saturday from 9:00 A.M. to 5:00 P.M. and Sunday from 1:00 to 5:00 P.M. Closed on Thanksgiving, Christmas, and New Year's Day. Planetarium shows are at 3:00 P.M. on Sunday; adults pay $2.00 for the show, children five and older, $1.00, plus museum entrance fee. Observatory hours, weather permitting, are 8:00 to 10:00 P.M. on Fridays; adults pay $3.00, children $2.00, with no museum entrance fee charged. The entrance fee to the Museum and Nature Center is $4.00 for adults, $3.00 for children five to thirteen, and no charge for children under five. For information, call 322–1646.

Just down the road from the Stamford Nature Center is the ever-beautiful **Bartlett Arboretum** (151 Brookdale Road), a sixty-three-acre sanctuary of natural-growth oak, maple, and hickory trees interspersed with evergreens, ash, birch, beech, and yellow poplar.

Five miles of trails lead visitors through woodlands, wetlands, and gardens. A reflecting pond at the end of the Woodland Trail is a perfect destination for young children, as is the boardwalk that leads through the unique Swamp Trail. The Ecology Trail combines portions of each of these trails. Pick up a guide book at the visitor center so you can better appreciate the twenty-seven marked stations.

On our most recent visit, we were delighted to find a nature activity backpack specially equipped for children under twelve to borrow. Crayons, scratch pads, a magnifying glass, and a wonderful set of cards with games, questions, activity suggestions, and educational information enhance the experience for the whole family. Borrow a backpack in the visitor center shop before you set out on a walk. After your walk, stop again at the visitor center. It contains a very good shop of garden and nature books, toys, games, and gifts, an exhibition hall, an ecology research laboratory, and a library of horticultural materials.

Guided walks are free to the public, as are Sunday concerts held approximately every other week during July and August (call for a schedule; pack a picnic supper to enjoy on the lawn as you listen). The Arboretum grounds are open free of charge from 8:30 A.M. to sunset every day of the year. The visitor center is open 8:30 A.M. to 4:00 P.M., Monday through Friday, except on holidays. Call 322–6971.

WESTPORT

Westport usually needs no introduction. A haven for writers, actors, artists, and other glitterati, it is well-known as the suburb of suburbs with a dash of panache rivaled only by its imitators. Though crowded with vehicle traffic, it still beckons with the same old zing. You can't miss the shops and restaurants—just follow the crowds. For other pleasures, follow our lead.

Start at the **Nature Center for Environmental Activities** at 10 Woodside Lane. Open 365 days a year from dawn to dusk, its sixty-two-acre wildlife sanctuary includes 3 miles of trails especially easy for the very young. A Swamp Loop Trail, an open field habitat, and a trail for the blind are among the outdoor options.

Inside the center's 20,000–square-foot museum, a live-animal hall with many species of indigenous animals is often the site of demonstrations. A Discovery Room with natural science artifacts on seasonal themes includes an interactive wall with changing displays on ecology and animal biology. A working water-quality lab, a wildlife rehab center, a variety of dioramas and aquariums, a marine touch tank, and a gift shop are here as well.

Workshops, guided walks, outdoor classes, summer camp programs, and special events like beachwalks, maple sugaring, birdbanding, and Earth Day activities are open to all visitors. Some are free; others require reservations and tuition. Come to this little slice of wilderness—wild turkeys, pheasants, red foxes, deer, hawks, songbirds, and more await you. Visit Monday through Saturday from 9:00 A.M. to 5:00 P.M. and Sunday from 1:00 to 4:00 P.M. Adults are invited to donate $1.00; children, 50 cents. For information, call 227–7253.

If you're looking for a beach, head to **Sherwood Island State Park,** right off I–95's exit 18. Turn south at the end of the ramp, and when you hit sand, you're there. Seriously, the 1½-mile beach is preceded by fields, picnic groves, and a variety of drives and footpaths. Swimming, fishing, scuba diving, and snorkeling are permitted in the Sound (divers must register at the Ranger Station); leave inflatable toys, boats, canoes, or kayaks at home. Lifeguards are on duty from Memorial Day to Labor Day.

Come here with your own equipment for kite-flying, volleyball, badminton, horseshoes, bocce, and bicycling. A softball field can be used on a first-come/first-play basis. On weekdays in the summer a model plane association has permission to use the park; visitors are welcome to watch their aerobatics.

Three recent additions to the park have enhanced its appeal to families. A sixteen-station self-guided interpretive nature trail points out flora, fauna, and areas of interest to Long Island Sound, its estuaries, and its shoreline. Just a half-mile long, it is perfect for families with young children and is informative for all ages. Secondly, a small nature center celebrating the marine environment includes a touch tank, live-animal exhibits of native reptiles and amphibians, some shorebird specimens, and other changing displays. The nature center is open from Memorial Day to Labor Day, except Mondays. Lastly, a bird observation deck provides an overview of the shore habitat; bird-watchers are welcome year-round. Interpretive naturalist-guided walks and talks are scheduled each season.

The park provides restrooms, changing rooms, and showers at no charge. Only the restrooms are open in winter. The concession stand is open only from Memorial Day to Labor Day. Folks are welcome to picnic or barbecue. Alcohol is permitted but not encouraged. Don't arrive with a keg for your family reunion—you will be asked to remove it from the park.

The park is open daily year-round from 8:00 A.M. to sunset. Admission per car is $5.00 for Connecticut vehicles and $8.00 for out-of-state vehicles from Memorial Day to Labor Day on weekdays and on weekends in May and September. On weekends and holidays from Memorial Day to Labor Day these respective rates are $7.00 and $12.00. Parking is free at all other times of the year. For information, call 226–6983.

For old-time summer stock theater, get tickets to the **Westport Country Playhouse** (25 Powers Court, just off Route 1). For over half a century, the playhouse has offered more than 700 productions starring such legends as Henry Fonda, Helen Hayes, Jessica Tandy, Gene Kelly, Cicely Tyson, and many others. Once a cow-barn-turned-tanning-factory and now a rustic post-and-beam country theater with red-cushioned bench-style seating, the playhouse is a Fairfield County fixture and one of the few remaining professional stock theaters in the Northeast.

The informal ambience of the theater is no reflection on the quality of the productions; in fact, it adds to the attraction. Six shows per season bring musicals, comedies, dramas, and classics to the stage. The summer series is not billed as family fare, but many productions are indeed suitable for the entire family.

Be sure to call for a schedule of the theater's children's summer series. For nine weeks every summer, a new show is performed each week on Fridays at 10:30 A.M. and 1:00 P.M. Fairy tale productions, a mini-circus, puppet theaters, magic shows, and concerts are among the possibilities. Tickets are fairly priced at $6.00 each for children and adults. Subscriptions are available to all shows. For information and reservations, call 226–0153 or 227–4177.

If even those prices are too high for your budget (and even if they are not), don't miss the festival atmosphere at the **Levitt Pavilion for the Performing Arts.** Right on the banks of Saugatuck River, the Levitt has offered approximately sixty evenings of entertainment every summer, from late June through late August, for the past twenty-two years. Bring a blanket and a picnic to the lawn in front of the bandshell and enjoy the absolutely free performances suitable for the whole family. Traditionally, Tuesday is Potpourri—maybe dance, country, or Big Band. Wednesday is Family Night Out (theater, mime, puppetry, magic, storytelling, singalongs). Thursday is Classical Joys, Friday is T.G.I.F. (maybe folk, bluegrass, or classic rock and roll), Saturday is Rock, and Sunday is Jazz. On Monday, there is no show.

A food/ice cream concession operates on some nights, but most folks bring picnic fare. Our family has enjoyed many an evening here—the performances aren't lengthy, but they make for a great night out.

Show times vary from 7:00 P.M. to as late as 8:30 P.M., but pre-show music is piped in from 6:30 P.M. to curtain time. Park in the municipal lot in back of the Westport Public Library on Jesup Road off the Post Road East (Route 1) and walk up the gravel path toward the bandshell at the side of the river. Call 226–7600 for a calendar or information.

Just in case you didn't find the shops and restaurants on your own, you ought to know about an educational/scientific/wonders-of-all-kinds shop called **Age of Reason** on the corner of the Post Road East and Riverside Avenue just across the river from the Levitt. It's great—don't miss it. Call 226–8191.

For great food, beautiful flowers, freshest-ever produce, and gourmet everything, stop at **Hay Day Country Farm and Market,** on the Post Road East going toward Fairfield. This complex also includes a wonderful coffee bar and a pretty cafe.

We shop at the market mostly for the great peasant herb bread and the organic pastas and rice, but admittedly the bill sometimes exceeds the balance in my checkbook. Only kidding—but just barely. The cafe serves excellent food beautifully prepared and graciously served. Maybe it was four sisters in pretty dresses that charmed the staff, but once we ate here for a graduation brunch and the servers did everything for our girls but give them manicures. They also have wonderful take-out items in the market. Call 221–0100.

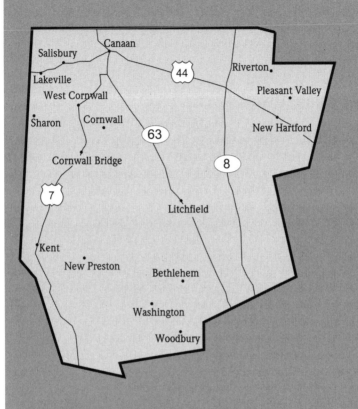

Salisbury
Canaan
Lakeville
West Cornwall
Riverton
44
Pleasant Valley
Sharon
Cornwall
63
New Hartford
Cornwall Bridge
8
7
Litchfield
Kent
New Preston
Bethlehem
Washington
Woodbury

Litchfield County

LITCHFIELD COUNTY

From its northwest corner where it meets the Berskhire Mountains to
the fertile valleys in the south formed by the Housatonic and
Farmington rivers, Litchfield County is famed for its beauty, history,
and prosperity. Punctuated by charming colonial towns, picturesque
lakes, and thousands of acres of forests and parks, it offers an intriguing
mix of rural and affluent culture. Resorts, restaurants, antiques shops, and
country inns draw visitors from all over to share in the wealth, while farmstands, potteries, church fairs, and nature preserves draw visitors eager to
taste the salt of the earth.

BETHELEM

Bethelem is Litchfield County at its best—gorgeous hills, a pretty village,
and quiet byways of unsurpassed serenity. No wonder that the inspiring
Benedictine nuns chose this place to build their beautiful **Abbey of
Regina Laudis.** Every summer in early August, the sisters open the gates
of the Abbey and welcome thousands upon thousands of visitors to share
in the bounteous festivities of their **Abbey Fair.**

Simple pleasures are heaped one upon the other in a splendid two-
day outpouring of spirit and celebration. Moderately akin to a Renaissance
Festival, in mood at least, the fair spreads over acres of land farmed by the sisters and those who help them. Among the barns and along the pathways of

the Abbey are tents and tables brimming with fresh baked goods, barbecued chicken, handcrafted gifts and toys, used books, baskets, quilts, jars of honey, garlands of dried flowers, and much, much more. Face painting, pony rides, tractor-drawn hayrides, and planting and crafting activities provide entertainment for children. Take a hayride—a volunteer farm worker will explain the workings of the farm and the experience of living with the sisters.

Before you leave the grounds, take a walk to the Abbey's magnificent Neopolitan crêche, which illustrates the Nativity in a starlit scene of more than forty eighteenth-century figures. The Abbey is located on Flanders Road, just a jog off Route 61. For information on the fair, call the Abbey's Little Art Shop at 266–7637.

CANAAN/FALLS VILLAGE

For those of us who live near the crowded New York-to-Boston corridor of I–95, visiting Canaan is like traveling to another country—a very rural, quiet country. Somehow Canaan and the villages surrounding it soothe the soul. Especially soothing is Falls Village's **Music Mountain,** not a place exactly, but a festival. The nation's oldest continuous chamber music festival, it also features jazz and folk music on its picturesque grounds just off Route 7 in Falls Village.

The intimate and apparently acoustically perfect wooden concert hall seats 335 for performances on Saturday nights and Sunday afternoons from early June to mid-September. Tickets for adults are $15.00; student tickets cost $5.00. They may be purchased by mail, by telephone for credit-card payments, or at the box office on concert days. For a schedule and information, call 496–2596 or 824–7126.

If you need action, call **Riverrunning Expeditions** on Main Street in Falls Village. Open from March through October, they offer one- or two-day trips of whitewater or quiet water canoeing or rafting on the beautiful Housatonic River. Instruction and guides are available, as are rentals and sales of canoes, kayaks, rafts, and tubes. Open Tuesday through Sunday from 9:00 A.M. to 5:00 P.M. Call 824–5579.

For an old-time adventure the whole family will enjoy, take a ride on the **Housatonic Railway Company's** 17-mile line from Canaan's historic 1872 Union Station to West Cornwall/Cornwall Bridge. The steam-powered engines take passengers on daily round-trip excursions through the valley from Memorial Day through late October. Fall foliage attracts the most riders, but it's pretty in summer, too. As I said before, if you live downstate or in the city, you're going to think these pristine hills and woodlands are out of this world. You can smell the green. For rates and a schedule, call 824–0339. When you get back to Canaan, explore Union Station a bit. The oldest train station still in use in the United States, the restored building is on the National Register of Historic Places.

Every year for the past thirty, folks here have celebrated this heritage in a ten-day festival called **Canaan Railroad Days.** Usually held in the second and third weeks in July, the festivities include a flea market, an arts and crafts fair, an antique and classic car show, an antique train show, hot air balloon rides, fireworks, and food. For information, call 528–0879.

A day in Canaan definitely ought to include a meal at **Collins Diner** on Route 44 at Railroad Plaza. Dazzlingly blue and neon on the outside and gleaming stainless steel on the inside, this delightful classic built by the O. J. Mahoney Company in 1941 is one of five diners in the United States to be placed on the National Register of Historic Places.

Spinning round counter stools, a black-and-white marble counter, red-covered seats, stainless steel coat racks at the end of each booth, and thick ceramic plates create a time-warp ambience we just love.

Proprietor Mike Hamzy, his son Ameen, and their crew serve up just what you might expect: hot roast beef sandwiches, spaghetti and meatballs, fried chicken, clam strips, and so on. Breakfast, available any time, is hard to resist. Pancakes, french toast, homefries, eggs any way you like 'em, and all combinations thereof are quintessentially diner. By the way, no air-fluffed milkshakes are served here. Syrup, ice cream, milk, and a whir of the old Hamilton Beach bring you sixteen ounces of ecstasy served straight up in a stainless steel tumbler. Be there—it's great.

The diner is open continuously from Friday at 5:30 A.M. to Sunday at 7:00 P.M.; Monday, Tuesday, and Thursday from 5:30 A.M. to 5:30 P.M.; and Wednesday from 5:30 A.M. to 1:30 P.M. Call 824–7040.

CORNWALL/WEST CORNWALL/CORNWALL BRIDGE

In a roughly elliptical shape outlined by Routes 7, 128, and 4, you'll find the villages of Cornwall, West Cornwall, and Cornwall Bridge, with state parks and forests shouldering each of them. Visit West Cornwall on Route 128 if only to see Connecticut's finest and largest covered bridge. Built in 1837 of native oak, the **West Cornwall Bridge** is a beauty. I don't think anyone is too jaded to feel its magic as it leads you across the river and back in time. I wish I could have heard the clip-clop of horses' hooves instead of the rumble of my car wheels as we made our crossing.

The village here is lovely and very tiny. **Freshfields, An American Restaurant,** on Route 128 has a wonderful Sunday brunch and a dining room overlooking the bridge and nearby waterfall. Call 672–6601 for reservations. Across the street is the **Cornwall Bridge Pottery Store,** which sells beautiful, lead-free stoneware crafted by its owner Todd Piker and other local artisans. Simon Pearce glassware, woodenware, leather goods, furniture, and other quality crafts are also sold here.

In Cornwall Bridge, 5 miles south on Route 7, visit the **Cornwall Bridge Pottery** itself and see the potters and wood-fired kiln at work. Todd Piker is owner, potter, philosopher, and excellent businessman. His pots (and plates, bowls, et cetera) are exceptionally beautiful and eminently useful. I suspect you'll love to see this process and so will the family. One of my daughters asked for a potter's wheel for her Christmas gift, so an impression must have been made. Call 672–6545.

One of the state's best campgrounds is in **Housatonic Meadows State Park** (just off Route 7). Right on the river, it offers plenty of opportunities for fishing and canoeing. Along one 2-mile stretch only fly-fishers are allowed. You can watch them or join them (the latter, only with a license). Cross-country skiing is popular in winter. One hundred campsites are available from mid-April through Columbus Day weekend. For information, call the park office at 927–3238 or the camp office at 672–6772.

In Cornwall, hit the slopes of **Mohawk Mountain Ski Area** in **Mohawk Mountain State Park** (Great Hollow Road, Route 4). Connecticut's largest ski area, it has twenty-four trails and slopes, six lifts, and snowmaking equipment for ninety-five percent of the slopes. Day and night skiing, rentals, lessons, snowmobiling, and cross-country skiing are all offered. In summer, mountain-biking, hiking, and picnicking draw thousands of visitors each year. You can call 672–6100 for more information.

A climb to the wooden observation tower at Mohawk Mountain's 1,683-foot summit will leave you speechless, not from the exercise but from the view. The rangers will give you a map and directions to the trailhead. Mohawk does not offer campsites, but a food concession, toilets, and picnic tables make for great daytripping.

KENT

I don't believe there's a family today who won't find something to please every member in the beautiful town of Kent. Start your day or weekend at **Kent Falls State Park,** right on Route 7 about 5 miles north of Kent's center. It's a great place to picnic, so you might want to stop at Kenk Natural Grocery on Route 7 between the center of Kent and the State Park. They sell organic fruits and vegetables, freshly made juices, and snacks made with no salt or wheat. They may not have everything you'll need, but what they do have is great.

Once at the park, you'll leave your car at the parking lot right off Route 7 at the base of a wide meadow that slopes down from the hills above. Beyond the meadow are the beautiful cascades of Kent Falls. Beginning in the town of Warren, the mountain stream known as Falls Brook reaches Kent through a series of drops, about 200 feet in total. Each drop is as pretty as the last as the falls descend through a dense forest of hemlocks, creating pools and potholes that openly invite visitors to dip a toe or even more into the cold, clear water.

Two trails to the top of the falls are cut through the forest on either side of the stream. We suggest you climb up the quarter-mile south trail directly to the right of the falls and descend on the north trail, which you reach by crossing the bridge at the top of the south trail. The trails are fairly steep at points, but small children will manage well if they rest from time to time. Stairs and railings on the south trail help those who haven't had a workout in a while. The slightly longer north trail angles off into the woods a bit away from the falls. You'll miss a pretty walk through the woodlands if you don't come down this way.

"Swimming" in the strictest sense is prohibited here, but wading or bathing (in bathing suits, please) in designated areas is absolutely allowed. Where else will you have a chance to cavort directly under a waterfall? The deepest pool may be waist- or even chest-high for adults, so don't take your eyes off small children if you're not going in with them. Wading, for them, may be very close to swimming in at least two of the pools. After you cool off, try some fishing in the stream as it nears the base of the meadow. The stream is stocked with trout, and no license is necessary for children under sixteen. Picnic tables and grills are scattered throughout the meadow and under the trees. Toilets are also available. You have to pack out your own trash, so be prepared. The park is open April 1 to December 1. A $5.00 parking fee is charged on weekends and holidays. For information, call 927–3238.

Back down Route 7 toward the village, you'll see signs for the **Sloane–Stanley Museum,** which sounds like another old-house tour but is not. Stop here for a look at one of the most surprisingly moving exhibits we've seen in the state. But it's weird—this collection is, well, it's . . . *tools.* Gathered through the efforts of author/artist Eric Sloane, the collection includes tools made by colonial Americans as early as the seventeenth century.

Their importance as a collection is fairly obvious and appealing, especially to children willing to guess the use of each object. Revealing much about the early settlers' adaptation to their new home, the tools are fascinating both in their diversity and ingenuity. They are also fascinating in their beauty. Finely crafted, mostly by hand, primarily from the hardwoods of the eastern woodlands, each object has been placed or hung and lighted by Sloane himself in a more artful way than even seems possible. The presence of each cabinetmaker, each farmer, each cook seems to fill the gorgeous post-and-beam barn in which the collection is housed.

The museum also includes a re-creation of Eric Sloane's art studio along with some of his original works. Outside the museum is a small cabin built by Sloane in 1974 with the use of notations found in an 1805 diary. The simple realities of frontier life are made obvious throughout the austere interior of this display. In addition, a visit to the ruins of the Kent Iron Furnace also on the property may have some interest. Long important

A dip under the falls at Kent Falls State Park is a great way to while away a hot summer afternoon. (Photo by the author)

as a producer of pig iron, the blast furnace is only partially restored. A diorama inside the museum explains the process of smelting pig iron and shows how the blast furnace would have worked.

The museum is open Wednesday through Sunday, 10:00 A.M. to 4:00 P.M. from mid-May to October 31. Adult admission is $3.00; children under twelve are $2.00. Call 927–3849.

Head back into town for a stroll through the shops on Route 7. All lovely, some are especially suited to families. **Folkcraft Instruments** (927–4492) sells smooth-as-silk harps, dulcimers, and hammered dulcimers handcrafted on the premises. These folks can teach some folks how to play the dulcimer in ten minutes. I managed "Go Tell Aunt Rhody" in about twelve minutes, but I'm working on improving my time.

For reasonably priced breakfasts and lunches in a welcoming family-style restaurant, go to **The Villager** (927–3945). Good soup, and club sandwiches a few inches tall are just some of what you'll find on their traditional roadside-diner menu. Open 6:00 A.M. to 4:00 P.M. Monday through Friday, 7:00 A.M. to 3:00 P.M. on Saturday, and 8:00 A.M. to 2:00 P.M. on Sunday.

If you hit town too late to get to the Villager, just do what we did—go to **Stroble Baking Company** (927–4073) for breads, baguettes, pastries, cakes, cookies, and coffee, and then stop by **Stosh's New England's Own Ice Cream** (927–4495) for the best ice cream in Litchfield County, if not anywhere. Try Turtle in a Puddle—pure pleasure. You can also buy sandwiches, muffins, drinks, and Dazzle Dogs—all-beef franks served on home-baked toasted buttered buns, plain or topped with good stuff. The buns are hands-down delicious, and the fat, juicy dogs, spicier than most kids like, are excellent adult-style wieners.

Your last stop in Kent might be **Macedonia State Park,** 4 miles north of the village off Route 341. With 2,300 acres, this park has excellent trails offering spectacular views of the Catskill and Taconic mountains. Camping, fishing, picnicking, and cross-country skiing are also available here. Take the trail to Cobble Mountain for a view you won't forget. It's just a half-mile to the top, then a mile down on another trail, or you can retrace the way you came. Ask a ranger for a map and trail condition information. For camping or other information, call 927–3238.

LITCHFIELD

One of the prettiest towns in the state, Litchfield attracts visitors in droves to its undisturbed colonial architecture, its boutiques, and its restaurants. It seems an area more suited to adults than to families, but we discovered a few places everyone should visit.

You can easily spend a whole day at the **White Memorial Foundation and Conservation Center Museum** at 80 Whitehall Road, 2 miles west of Litchfield Center off Route 202. The state's largest nature preserve with 4,000 acres and 35 miles of trails, White Memorial is a wonderful place to hike, horseback ride, cross-country ski, fish, and picnic. Two family campgrounds offer lakeside or woodland sites, and a public boat launch provides access to Bantam Lake. A bird observatory overlooks a specially landscaped area attractive to many bird species. Thirty sheltered viewing stations have been created for bird-watchers and photographers. The Trail of the Senses is an especially lovely short interpretive walk that's excellent for young children. You might also want to sign up for a special program, take a guided walk, or visit on the annual Family Nature Day in late September. Birdbanding, tree identification, outdoor games, a pond life study, and much more are offered at this popular event.

Make certain that you go to the Conservation Center Museum, an excellent hands-on nature center with appeal for all ages. Dioramas and interactive exhibits on birds, bees, soil, seeds, woodland animals, and more are artistically arranged in a bright, open atmosphere. An outstanding natural science library is open even to daytripping visitors, with a children's section so comfortable it practically invites you to sit down and read.

The White Memorial grounds are open seven days a week, year-round, from dawn to dusk. Admission is free. The museum is open daily as well, from 9:00 A.M. to 5:00 p.m., Monday through Saturday and on Sunday from noon to 4:00 P.M. Adult admission to the museum is $1.50; children under twelve pay 75 cents. For information, call 567–0857.

If you want to take a dip in pretty Bantam Lake, leave Litchfield Center on Route 202 West, take a left on White's Woods Road, and another right on East Shore Road. Just before the bend in the road, you'll find the entrance to **Sandy Beach.** Actually in the town of Morris, the secluded beach provides 800 feet of clean sand on the shore of Connecticut's largest natural lake.

Lifeguards, bathrooms and bathhouses, and a snack bar are among the amenities. A canoe launch, a volleyball "court," and a picnic area with tables and fire pits make this a great place to spend the day. If you're a good swimmer, you can swim out to the raft; it has a terrific slide that sweeps you right into the cool, clear water.

Open to the public on weekends only from Memorial Day through the end of June, the beach is open daily from late June through Labor Day, from 9:00 A.M. to 7:00 P.M. The cost per car or boat is $5.00 per visit; the cost for each bicycler or walker is $1.00. Nonresident season passes are $60.00 per family. For information, call 567–9461.

If horses or horseback riding interest you, go directly to **Lee's Riding Stable** at 57 East Litchfield Road. One-hour guided trail rides on registered Morgan horses are $22 per person. Groups are normally limited to six to eight riders, so you don't get that mule-train feeling. Visitors are welcome anytime; reservations for trail rides are preferred but not absolutely necessary. The property is adjacent to Topsmead State Forest, and the trails take you through some exceptionally pretty country.

Pony rides in an outdoor ring are $3.50 for twice-around-the ring or $11.00 for a half-hour parent-guided ride. If the staff is not too busy, they'll give you a tour of the stables and pastures. Riding lessons are also offered. A new indoor ring is used in bad weather and for therapeutic riding for the handicapped (call for information if you're interested). Birthday parties, longer outings, and custom group rides can all be arranged. Lee's is open 365 days a year. The horses are beauties, and Lee Lyons, who runs the whole show, has a down-to-earth approach that makes everyone feel welcome and comfortable. For information, call 567–0785.

If you're tuckered out after all these outdoor activities, we suggest a quiet browse through the **Cobble Court Bookshop** at 10 Cobble Court in the center of Litchfield. It's hard to leave this lovely store, but you may be enticed to refresh yourself at **Doyle's Ice Cream Parlor** nearby on the corner of the Green. Sixteen flavors may not sound like a lot to choose from, but they are each as good as ice cream can be. The old-fashioned atmosphere may inspire you to order an old-time fountain treat—I can vouch for the root-beer floats. Open from 9:00 A.M to 9:00 P.M. daily,

Doyle's (567–0516) has some healthy (depending on your view of ice cream) competition at **Peaches 'n Cream Ice Cream** (632 Torrington Road). Also open all year, these folks offer more flavors but a little less ambience. We won't tell you which we think is better—you be the judge. Call Peaches 'n Cream at 496–7536.

If you haven't tired of history lessons, have a look at the impressive collections of the **Litchfield Historical Society,** at the corner of East and South streets. For hours and information, call 567–4501. Likewise, you might want to stop at the **Tapping Reeve House and Law School** on South Street to inspire future attorneys to emulate the 130 members of Congress who graduated from this first law school in the nation, now open to the public as a historical exhibit. For hours and admission information, call the Historical Society at 567–4501.

NEW HARTFORD

You might like to know what we liked best of all the adventures we had researching this book. Well, this next adventure is certainly on our top-twenty list of best family activities in Connecticut—that is, if you're ten years or older and can swim alone without a doubt. Tubing down the Farmington River from **Satan's Kingdom State Recreation Area** in New Hartford is fun. That's all, folks—it's just fun. We did it last year on the Fourth of July, and the river was chock-full of other tubing enthusiasts; we did it midweek in June and were alone except for the dragonflies.

It works like this: You drive to Satan's Kingdom on Route 44 and you park in the large lot right next to the river and the **North American Canoe Tours, Inc.** (NACT) outpost. Wear your cut-offs and a T-shirt to the place or change in one of the very poorly lit changing huts provided at the lot. (You can go shirtless or wear a bathing suit, but sunburn and a lifevest go together like sandpaper and skin.) Put on some old sneakers, preferably your own. If you arrive barefoot, NACT is going to make you put on one of their spare pairs of soggy previously owned sneaks. Put on your sunscreen and put on your lifevest. (The lifevest is mandatory equipment for everyone.) Now pay your $9.00 (or $7.00 if you're in a group of ten or more who have called at least a day ahead for reservations). Now put your warm body into the cold water, bottom first, as you sit down in the hole of your tube with your feet up over the side. Sound like fun yet? It is, really—I promise. Now all you have to do is float and soak up the vitamin D rays for 2½ miles in about equally as many hours.

The best parts for some are the mild rapids—three sets, with NACT lifeguards on duty in kayaks; others like the placid stretches where mergansers nest and the living is easy. Open every day from mid-June to Labor Day and on weekends only from Memorial Day to mid-June and Labor Day to the end of September, NACT rents tubes from 10:00 A.M. to approximately 5:00 P.M. When your ride is over (at a marked take-out point), haul out, and a shuttle bus will take you back to the starting point. Call 693–6465.

NEW PRESTON

To be brief for reasons of space alone, I'd just like to mention **Lake Waramaug State Park** and the **Inn at Lake Waramaug.** To start with the basics, Waramaug is the Indian word for "good fishing place." If you're so inclined, this sounds like the best fishing tip I've ever heard. You might also want to know that the Lake Waramaug area is often compared to European alpine lake regions. Certainly its beauty ranks it among the loveliest of all destinations in Connecticut. Located on Lake Waramaug Road (Route 478) 5 miles north of New Preston Center, the park offers fishing, scuba diving, sailing, swimming, and paddle boats and canoes (to rent). Hiking trails and eighty-eight campsites are also available. Ice-skating, cross-country skiing, and ice fishing are possible in winter. Call the park office at 868–2592 or the campground office at 868–0220.

At 107 North Shore Road in New Preston is the Inn at Lake Waramaug. An excellent family inn with tastefully decorated rooms in an enormous 1790s colonial, it's expensive but wonderful. Among its outstanding features are its annual events open at no charge to the public and perfect for families. In February, the Ice Harvest and Winter Fun Festival has contests for best snowman, best snow sculpture, and best ice-carving. A demonstration of ice harvesting on the lake shows how it was done "in the olden days." In March, a Maple Sugaring Time Festival demonstrates sugar maple tapping and syrup making. Everyone gets a taste, and maple products are for sale. In July, at the Old-Fashioned Frog Jump Jamboree, children under sixteen enter their frogs in a race in which the frogs have no interest. The object is to convince the frogs to leap the longest distance for prizes the kids win. Among the handful of other special events, our favorite is the Huckleberry Finn Raft Race on Labor Day, when dozens of homemade watercrafts race to claim the coveted Huck Finn Cup. The race begins at 3:00 P.M. Contestants should arrive by 2:15 P.M. to register. Come soon just to watch or to participate. For information on events or reservations at the Inn, call (800) LAKE–INN. If you're hungry in New Preston, waste no time. Go straight to **Doc's Restaurant** on Lake Waramaug for the best pizza in Litchfield County. Call 868–9415.

RIVERTON/PLEASANT VALLEY

The Riverton area is just a plain old nice place to be. To be specific, the roughly rectangular region created by the roads linking Riverton, Pleasant Valley, Barkhamsted, and West Hartland is an area to which any world-weary family can go to restore some equilibrium. Start at **People's State Forest,** which nearly fills the aforementioned rectangle scribed loosely by Routes 318, 181, and 20 and cut further by the East and West River roads that flank the sides of the Farmington River's West Branch. East River Road will take you to the Forest's public entrance. A gorgeous grove overlooks the rushing water as it twists through the 200-year-old pines—stop here for lunch if you've packed a picnic. Anglers hip deep in the water during trout season are a pleasant addition to the majestic view.

Up in Riverton proper, stop the car and smell the roses. Figuratively speaking, that is. The **Riverton General Store** on Route 20 is a good place to begin your walk. Besides icy-cold I.B.C root beer, they have everything under the sun, including stuff manufactured before the turn of the century, settin' and hangin' left, right, and center. I never did ask if the great old stuff was for sale or just for display, but I do know that kids love this place. There's even a bear—I swear. They're open seven days a week from 6:00 A.M. to 8:00 P.M. Call 379–0811.

Down the side streets are a scattering of pretty shops in pretty houses and the surprisingly interesting **Hitchcock Chair Museum** (379–4826). I won't mislead you—the kids thought the chairs were pretty, like the shops and the houses, but they also wanted to know when we were going to the **Village Sweet Shop** for ice cream. And chocolate. "I don't even *like* chairs," one of them said. Still, we had family fun (and superior ice cream) in Riverton. The Sweet Shop, also on Route 20, is open from 10:00 A.M. to 5:00 P.M. Monday through Saturday and noon to 5:00 P.M. on Sunday. Call 379–7250.

Next year we're coming back for the annual **Riverton Fishing Derby** on opening day of fishing season in Connecticut (always the third Saturday in April). Prizes are awarded in adult and youth divisions of this classic event, held from 6:00 to 10:00 A.M. For information, call 263–2841. You can buy a fishing license right at the General Store.

SALISBURY/LAKEVILLE

Connecticut doesn't have a prettier town than Salisbury. They should place signs at the edge of the town that say PLEASE DO NOT DISTURB. A quiet corner of pure sanity, Salisbury is home to one of our family's favorite places. Just let me ask you this favor: Keep in mind the name of this operation and respect its special qualities of peace and harmony with the earth. A welcoming enclave of beauty, fragrance, and fun, **Sweethaven Farm** on Weatogue Road just a short distance off Route 44 specializes in growing organic herbs and flowers on the eight-acre property. Owner Noreen Driscoll Breslauer has created summer garden and craft workshops that allow boys and girls ages five and older to explore the world of the garden through stories, crafts, games, gardening, and cooking.

Children ages five through ten may enjoy the Peter Rabbit workshops held on six consecutive summer Wednesdays in and around the Beatrix Potter–Peter Rabbit garden. Delightfully guarded by scarecrow-style figures of Peter and his family, the garden is sowed with the herbs and flowers that appear in the illustrations of Potter's stories. Children may sign up for one or more or all of the sessions. Following the last session is a Beatrix Potter garden party for participants and their families. In late July a Peter Rabbit tea party is open to the public (call for reservations—last year 150 people came).

Older children may enjoy the Herb Craft Camp offered on Tuesdays and Thursdays. Herbal weavings, leaf printings, fabric dyes, wreathmaking, cooking, and planting are among the hands-on activities. Fees last year were $18 a day or $100 for all six sessions. Each session runs from 10:00 A.M. to 2:30 P.M. Participants should bring a healthy lunch from home. An afternoon basketry workshop is also given by Joann Catsos of Ashley Falls, Massachusetts. She leads children in making six different basket designs during her six-week course. Pre-registration is necessary for all classes, and they fill up quickly as class size is limited to ten to fourteen children. Other classes for adults and children are also offered throughout the year.

Sweethaven Farm has a wonderful barn shop full of herbal vinegars, potpourris, wreaths, culinary blends, topiaries, and more. Your children may want to say hello to Pinocchio the pony and Jezebel the goat while you shop. The barn and gardens are open to the public from 10:00 A.M. to 4:00 P.M. on Saturday during February, March, and April, and during the same hours on Friday through Sunday from May through December. To register for classes or for other information, call 824–5765.

The **Salisbury Cannon Museum at the Holley–Williams House** on Route 44 in the Lakeville section of Salisbury tells the story of the Revolutionary War and the cannon factory that operated in Lakeville in 1776. Using the nearly limitless supply of iron ore discovered in the surrounding hills, the factory made cannon and cannonballs for Washington's army as well as Connecticut privateers defending the seacoast against British vessels. The museum describes the unglorified but essential roles of seven historic individuals who contributed to America's fight for independence. The story of each person begins on April 19, 1775, the day the first shot of the war was fired on Lexington Green. Children can also heft cannonballs made during the Revolution and dress up in a kid-sized Revolutionary War uniform.

For information on the hours of and admission to this brand-new exhibit, call the Holley–Williams House at 435–2878. Tours of the Holley–Williams House are given by appointment year-round. The schedule may change as more visitors are attracted to the excellent exhibits of the Cannon Museum, which is in the Holley–Williams Carriage House.

More famous than these by far is Lakeville's **Lime Rock Park,** "the road racing center of the East." Family adventure? I guess so, but I'm the wrong person to ask. My racing aficionado brother-in-law says yes. Near the junction of Routes 7 and 112, the racetrack offers world-class sports-car and stock-car racing from April through October. Events are open to the public on Saturdays and holidays. Come here for the annual Memorial Day Grand Prix, the Formula Ford Festival and Fireworks on the Fourth of July weekend, and the BMW Vintage Fall Festival on Labor Day weekend. For tickets and information, call 435–0896 or (800) RACE–LRP.

SHARON

Route 4 in the charming village of Sharon will bring you to the 684-acre **Sharon Audubon Center,** formerly called the Northeast Center. Like all of the Audubon Society's facilities, the center is exceptionally well done with carefully tended trails throughout several sorts of habitats. Pond, swamp, marsh, and woodland areas are clearly marked with self-guided interpretive nature walks planned for all habitats. Naturalist-guided walks are also offered for families or groups on a variety of topics—birds, trees, mammals, et cetera.

The center's main building includes natural science exhibits and an excellent gift and book shop. The children's Discovery Room has a feature we've not seen anywhere else: listening boxes in which to sit. Tapes triggered by the weight of children play sounds of whales, rainstorms, and more. Kids can crawl through a simulated beaver's den, identify skulls, look at a real honeybee hive, and more.

Outdoors is a wildlife rehabilitation center. Many animals reside here only temporarily, so you may see something new each time you come. Turtles, snakes, and birds are the most common species found here. If you come in spring or summer near evening or early morning, you may see the beavers at Ford or Bog Meadow ponds. Warblers tend to stop here on their annual migrations, so bird-watchers might enjoy a visit at those times.

The Audubon Center maintains an herb garden, a wildflower garden, and a new butterfly and hummingbird garden. A visit on the last full weekend in July will allow you to join the activities of the Annual Audubon Festival, featuring hands-on crafts for children, demonstrations, workshops, music, pony rides, and food. In addition, a summer day camp for children ages four through thirteen is offered every July and August.

Access to the trails costs $3.00 per adult and $1.50 per child. There is no charge to visit the center's main building, which is open year-round from Monday through Saturday, 9:00 A.M. to 5:00 P.M. and on Sunday from 1:00 to 5:00 P.M. For information on the wide variety of events and programs offered here, call 364–0520.

WASHINGTON

Don't blink or you'll miss this town hidden in the twists and turns of these lovely hills. As beautiful as its village is, the special treasure in Washington is the **Institute for American Indian Studies** on Curtis Road, off Route 199. Magnificently displayed in a discreet building smack-dab in the woodlands near Steep Rock Nature Preserve, the exhibits are interpretations of the Institute's research on the history and culture of Indian America. The permanent exhibit entitled *As We Tell Our Stories: Living Tradition and the Algonkian Peoples of New England,* includes the taped stories of Algonkian people and an extensive collection of Native American tools, baskets, implements, and art. A furnished reproduction longhouse is built inside the museum and is filled with artifacts used in everyday life. An excellent gift shop and two galleries of art are also inside.

Outside, an authentically constructed seventeenth-century settlement with three wigwams, a longhouse, a rock shelter, and a garden planted each season with corn, beans, and squash provides a peek into the proud 10,000-year history of these people. A simulated archaeological site offers intriguing insights into their moving story.

There's lots to learn here. Craft workshops, dances, films, storytelling, and more are on the annual events calendar. We attended a wonderful festival with a raptor demonstration, arts and crafts, and native foods. Children's summer camps are also on the schedule. Open year-round Monday through Saturday from 10:00 A.M. to 5:00 P.M. and Sunday from noon to 6:00 P.M. Adult admission is $4.00; children six to sixteen pay $2.00. For information, call 868–0518.

WOODBURY

Larger and more populated than many of Litchfield County's towns, Woodbury is a pleasant community with a great deal to offer daytripping families. Once known for its agriculture and its production of cutlery and cloth, Woodbury is now famed as the place to go for antiques.

Families wary of entering crowded shops of expensive goods may enjoy a trip to the child-friendly **Woodbury's Famous Antiques and Flea Market.** It's open every Saturday, April through December, from 7:00 A.M. to 4:00 P.M. Go early for the best selection or late for the best bargains. Antiques are well mixed with junk, and new stuff is well mixed with authentic collectibles. The outdoor market is held at the junction of Routes 6 and 64. Admission is free, as is parking. Call 263–2841.

Practically across the street, on Hollow Road just off Route 6, is the **Glebe House and Gertrude Jekyll Garden.** This 1745 minister's farmhouse, or glebe, is an exceptional example of eighteenth-century architecture and is especially welcoming to children. The mood inside the house is warm and inviting. Artifacts are laid out in positions of use, and children are enthusiastically addressed on tours tailored to the interests and schedule of the visitors. Historically important as the site of the first election of an American bishop of the Episcopal Church in 1783, the house has many fine (and simple) furnishings and a charming gift shop/bookstore. Its beautiful perennial garden is the only one in the United States designed by renowned English landscape designer Gertrude Jekyll.

Most importantly for interested families, the museum's curator, Brian MacFarland, hosts a History Camp for children ages eight to twelve every August. A week-long program of colonial activities, it is an eye-opening experience of eighteenth-century daily life. The program is so popular that three sessions were offered last year. Glebe House is open from 1:00 to 4:00 P.M. Wednesday through Sunday, from April through November, and is open by appointment December through March. The suggested donation is $3.00 per adult. For information, call 263–2855.

For outdoor sports enthusiasts, **Woodbury Ski and Racquet Area** offers a year-round recreational facility that attracts thousands of visitors each year. Its fourteen downhill trails are especially popular with children and with beginner and intermediate skiers. Lessons, rentals, and night skiing specials are offered, and a double chairlift, three tow ropes, and snowmaking equipment keep the pace active all season long. Twenty miles of groomed cross-country trails are also on the property. Snowboarding, sledding, tobogganing, and ice-skating provide lots of opportunities to have winter adventures. The area is open weekdays from 10:00 A.M. to 10:00 p.m., Saturdays from 9:00 A.M. to 10:00 p.m., and Sundays, 9:00 A.M. to 4:30 P.M. In the summer, you can swim, picnic, play tennis and paddle tennis, and go skateboarding.

You may want to go on the second Sunday of the month, May through September, to partake of the summer music festival held here for the past twenty-two years. Bluegrass, "country Cajun," rock, or reggae concerts are all-day (11:00 A.M. to 6:00 p.m.) affairs held in the natural outdoor amphitheater. Arts, crafts, and international foods are sold throughout each festival day. For festival ticket information and general information year-round, call 263–2203.

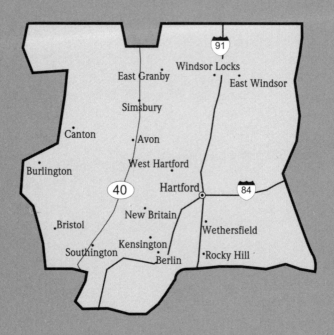

East Granby

Windsor Locks

East Windsor

Simsbury

Canton

Avon

West Hartford

Burlington

40

Hartford

84

New Britain

Wethersfield

Bristol

Kensington

Southington

Berlin

Rocky Hill

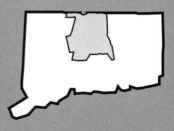

Hartford County

HARTFORD COUNTY

The north-central region of Connecticut is an area of diversity. Sliced into unequal parts by the Connecticut River, it includes farming communities, towns with a long history of industry, and a city of pre–Revolutionary War importance as a seat of government. This diversity makes for perfect touring conditions, as it offers something for all tastes, interests, and ages.

Hartford itself presents a full slate of attractions typical of an urban cultural center. The arts, sciences, history, and industries of the city, the state, and the nation are well represented in Hartford's museums, exhibits, and special events. In the surrounding towns, you will find attractions that reflect each community's unique history and importance. Defined by such tourist district names as Tobacco Valley or Olde Towne, every area of this county provides opportunities for family adventure.

AVON

Named for the river in Stratford, England, Avon originated in 1645 as a section of Farmington. First known as Nod, Avon grew substantially in the eighteenth century when the new stagecoach route from Boston to Albany ran through town. Along with the Albany Turnpike came prosperity for the farmers and traders of the region, who capitalized on the needs of the travelers passing through town. Inn- and tavern-keepers, blacksmiths and harnessmakers, merchants and even bandits—all benefitted from the construction of the road we now call Route 44.

Avon has retained all signs of the affluence it achieved in its past. Now a carefully groomed community populated largely by Hartford executives and professionals, it is plump with restaurants and shops catering to a comfortable clientele. For tourists, this means wonderful food and great shopping. Unfortunately, the kids might lose interest after a while.

No worry—Avon is home to more than a few places the kids might really enjoy, albeit with one caveat: It's best to be here in summer or fall. One such place is the **Avon Cider Mill** (57 Waterville Road, which is Route 10). From apples trucked in from upstate New York, the Lattizori brothers produce 35,000 to 40,000 gallons of cider every year, starting in mid-September. You can actually watch them make the cider in the press their grandfather bought in 1919, but you'd have to get up pretty early in the morning. Cider-making begins at 2:00 A.M. and is usually completed by 7:00 A.M. What you can more feasibly do, however, is visit their market throughout the season to sample the wonderful variations of the cider as the weather changes. The sweetest cider comes late in the season (October-ish), and it is also at that time that the apple fritter man sets up his cart near the market and turns out fresh, hot fritters, melt-in-your-mouth cider doughnuts, and hot spiced cider.

The market sells apples, baked goods, pumpkins, and fall accoutrements like Indian corn, gourds, mums, and more. Later in the season, they truck in the Christmas trees. After the holiday, the Lattizoris get to rest a bit; they close shop until spring, when they bring out plants for your gardens. The Mill is open daily in season from 9:00 A.M. to 5:00 P.M. Call 677–0343.

In the same vein, only more so, you might like to stop by the **Pickin' Patch,** just a mile and a half up Nod Road, which begins at the Avon Old Farms Inn at the corner of Routes 10 and 44. Owned by Janet and Don Carville, the farm has been in Mrs. Carville's family since 1666 when her ancestors, the Woodfords, came from Hartford after accompanying founding father Thomas Hooker to Connecticut. Proud of her ancestry (two of her relatives pounded in the nails of the Avon Congregational Church), Mrs. Carville is a fountain of information on area history.

Her farm is also a fountain of other riches, namely nearly everything growing under the sun from asparagus to zucchini. As the name suggests, this is a pick-your-own place, operating from roughly mid-April to December until the Christmas trees are gone and they turn the lights out on Christmas Eve. The tenth oldest family farm in Connecticut, the Pickin' Patch grows the largest variety of berries, vegetables, and flowers in the state. Strawberries, blackberries, blueberries, peas, cucumbers, tomatoes, peppers, and more are sold at half the cost of retail if you pick the crops yourself. Call the number below for crop information.

Absolutely beautiful when the fall foliage is at its peak, the joint really starts hopping when pumpkin season and the hayrides begin. On Saturdays and Sundays in October from 10:00 A.M. to 5:00 p.m., you can ride the tractor-driven haywagons out to the fields to pick your own pumpkins. If you go between 2:00 and 4:00 p.m., you may meet the Pumpkin Lady, who walks out to the fields to greet the children. In December, also on Saturdays and Sundays from 2:00 to 4:00 p.m., a fully lit and decorated Christmas Tree walks among the real ones, greeting the surprised children on cut-your-own outings. The farm is open daily from 8:00 A.M. to 6:00 P.M. You're welcome anytime to see what's growing, but there's not much action after Christmas. Stop by in April when the greenhouses open. Hardy annuals and perennials, including dig-your-own mums, are for sale through the growing season. For information, call 677–9552.

Located just under a half-mile west of the junction of Routes 44 and 10 North in a complex called Avon Park North is the **Farmington Valley Arts Center.** Turn from Route 44 onto Ensign Drive, then left onto Arts Center Lane. The second and third buildings slightly askew at your left are the Arts Center buildings. Former factory buildings, these century-old brownstone structures now house the twenty studios that comprise the Center.

Painting, ceramics, weaving, and sculpture are just a few of the media explored here by artists and students. Classes are offered for children and adults at every level—beginners as well as advanced. Artists work on individual schedules, but there is almost always someone here to watch. You are welcome to stroll from studio to studio throughout the year, especially Wednesday through Sunday from February through October or seven days a week in November and December. Open Arts Day in early

June is a festival event with demonstrations, classes, musicians, dancers, a theater performance, and other entertainments related to the arts.

From the first Saturday in November until Christmas Eve, the Arts Center's annual holiday exhibit features strolling musicians, luminaria, and other festivities on opening night, plus sales of contemporary American crafts thereafter in the Fisher Gallery, the FVAC store. Open year-round Wednesday through Saturday from 11:00 A.M. to 5:00 P.M. and on Sunday from noon to 4:00 p.m., the shop is the best of its kind I have seen in the state—a varied collection of pottery, jewelry, toys, prints, clothing, and other exceptional crafts. As you pass the FVAC office on your way to the gallery or the studios, stop by and ask for a course catalog. The teen and children's summer classes at the Learning Center Annex are wonderful. If you haven't time for a whole course, try one of the Family Arts Days sessions held twice each summer for family groups. Call 678–1867.

BERLIN

South of New Britain is the town of Berlin, just off the Berlin Turnpike (U.S. Highway 15 and State Highway 5). Driving either north or south on the Turnpike, you can't help but see **Safari Golf** high on the western side of the road. Recently voted the best miniature golf course in the Hartford area by the readers of the *Hartford Advocate,* the golf course is, in our family's opinion, the best in the state. Themed miniature golf courses seem to be the newest tack in the business, giving the entertainment new life and increasing its attraction for families. Safari Golf has a jungle motif complete with life-sized statues of African animals. A clutch of giraffes grazes on a hillside, a mother rhinoceros with her baby rambles out of the forest, monkeys swing from the trees. A herd of zebras, a gorilla family, and a large lion share the property with the herons and elephants who frequent the waterhole.

Wide walkways lead players around the course, which is well lighted and in extremely good repair. In fact, Safari Golf is more beautifully landscaped than some exhibition gardens I've seen. A lighted waterfall and a bubbling stream add to the drama. African-style huts provide a place to rest or wait throughout the course, and a party deck with tables can be used for birthday parties or picnics.

You can play free on your birthday and special values are offered to your guests. Hours are extensive, but they change seasonally. For information, call 828–9800.

BRISTOL

Though firmly in Hartford County, the small industrial city of Bristol is classified by the State Tourism Commission as part of Litchfield Hills. The city's history as a center of venerable Yankee industries, however, gives it a distinctive character much more in line with Hartford than Litchfield.

In honor of those industrious craftsmen, you might start a day in Bristol at the **American Clock and Watch Museum** at 100 Maple Street. More than 3,000 ticking, striking, and chiming clocks and watches are beautifully displayed in a nineteenth-century colonial home that has two modern wings filled with the largest of the clocks.

A forest of grandfather clocks in one wing includes a 10-foot-tall behemoth that strikes twice each quarter-hour. A representation of an eighteenth-century wooden-works clock shop is also in this wing, complete with ledger books, manuals, and clocks in various stages of finishing. Back in the main house, a charming clock shop is re-created with hundreds of clocks that would have been sold in the 1890s, including the original fixtures from an actual 1890s shop in Plymouth, Connecticut.

The collection is magnificent and very appealing to children. We found clocks shaped like Old King Cole, a bumblebee, a frying pan, a pumpkin, a violin, a town crier . . . the list could go on and on. The museum also contains the largest collection of Hickory Dickory Dock clocks anywhere. Eight of them are here, with a running mouse, of course, on each one. Children may enjoy finding Mickey Mouse, Bugs Bunny, Barbie, and other characters among the beautiful antique cabinet clocks, pocket watches, and wristwatches.

Stroll out to the courtyard perennial garden and ask a docent to ring the huge bronze bell for you. Don't say we didn't warn you to cover your ears. The museum is open daily from March 1 through November 30 except for Thanksgiving, from 10:00 A.M. to 5:00 P.M. Adult admission is $3.50; children under fifteen pay $1.50. For information, call 583–6070.

At the **New England Carousel Museum** (95 Riverside Avenue, which is Route 72) you can visit one of the nation's largest displays of antique carousel pieces. The golden age of the carousel from 1880 through the 1930s is portrayed in this restored hosiery mill—the "Stockingnet Factory"—that houses both the museum and the restoration workshop of carousel expert Bill Finkenstein.

The main hall contains a constantly changing parade of figures so colorful and stately that one cannot help but be drawn into their magic. Many of the horses have been rescued from demolition and restored here. Most are on long-term loan from private collectors, a situation that infuses the museum with new life each time an exhibit is brought in. Coney Island, Philadelphia, and Country Fair styles are represented in their spectacular original colors and elaborate trappings. The simplicity of the hall underscores the grandeur of the horses, chariots, band organs, and rounding boards. You can't help but smile and you might even feel like dancing when you hear the beautiful band organ music that fills the hall.

Tour guides tailor their talks to the ages and interests of the visitors. Children are invited to feel a horsehair tail and to guess at various details of carousel construction. A re-creation of a carver's workshop reveals the secrets of the craft; the particular details of famed master carvers such as Illions, Stein and Goldstein, Denzel, and Looff are pointed out.

Come often—displays change frequently. When we were here a marvelous Wurlitzer band organ was as well, but now it's gone back home so the museum can bring in for winter storage the forty-nine horses, one boat, two chariots, and band organ of the Lake Compounce Carousel.

The museum may make you ache for a carousel ride, but you can't do it here. Luckily, you're in a great state for carousels. Although by the turn of the century more than 3,000 carousels operated in the United States, fewer than one hundred still exist. Connecticut is home to three of these, plus a few new ones like the carousels in the Danbury Fair Mall (see page 7) and at Lake Quassapaug (see page 97). Of the three antiques, two are currently operating, and we test-rode them for you in Hartford and New Haven (see pages 67 and 101 respectively). The other is in storage in Bridgeport, and soon you will be able either to ride the restored antique or just look at it on display while you ride a reproduction in the brand-new

Carousel House at Beardsley Zoological Park (see page 5).

Call for information on the museum's Painted Pony Pajama Parties, evening or sleepover programs that include crafts, games, storytelling, a tour of the museum, and snack or breakfast. The museum is open year-round Monday through Saturday from 10:00 A.M. to 5:00 P.M. and Sunday from noon to 5:00 P.M. It is closed on New Year's Day, Easter Sunday, Independence Day, Labor Day, Thanksgiving, Christmas, and Mondays from November through March. Adult admission is $4.00; children under fourteen pay $2.50. For information, call 585–5411.

If the joyful noise of the band organ doesn't make your spirits soar, **Balloons Over Bristol** will. An annual event held every Memorial Day weekend, it centers on the launching of up to sixty hot air balloons from the fields of Eastern Regional High School on Route 229. Balloonists from all over the United States gather, weather permitting, to go up at 6:00 A.M. and 6:00 P.M. on Saturday and Sunday.

Once a simple gathering of hundreds of awed folks and aficionados on the field, it is now, nearly twenty years later, a traffic-stopping, fullblown festival of food, crafts (not juried), air-balloon souvenirs, and kiddie rides and activities. To be honest, we liked it better the old way. We still pack a wicker basket with chicken salad sandwiches, throw down a quilt on the grass, and wait for the glorious flight of these beautiful birds. Let the others eat fried dough; we're here for the balloons.

Fair warning: When the balloons go up, it's amazingly beautiful, but when it's too windy or looking too much like rain, it's downright disappointing. No one goes up at all. We take a vote every year to see who thinks it's worth the risk, and we always go. For information, call 585–7755.

If you have nothing to do between lift-offs, you might visit the **H. C. Barnes Nature Center and Preserve** (175 Shrub Road). The small seventy-acre sanctuary is lovely and features great walking trails for children. The Nature Center has several "please touch" centers with a variety of natural objects to explore and handle. Several species of live animals reside here, including a black rat snake named Max, which one of our daughters wore around her neck for some time, much to our surprise.

If you're from the area you may want to pick up one of their brochures listing programs offered to kids. The trails are open dawn to dusk year-round. The center is open from 9:00 A.M. to 5:00 P.M. Monday through Friday. For information, call 585–8886.

BURLINGTON

We wouldn't even have known Burlington existed if it weren't for an intriguing sign near Nassahegon State Forest that essentially said "trout hatchery that-a-way." When we saw it again on a state map published by a V.I.P. map company, we thought we'd check it out. Sure enough, the **Burlington Trout Hatchery** exists big-time and is open to the public year-round.

Inside the main building are incubation trays for eggs and long race-ways filled with fingerlings, sorted by age. Outside are the nursery, breeder, and rearing pools, as well as production ponds for all the stages of raising brown trout, sock-eye salmon, brook trout, and rainbow trout. After they reach 9 inches or so, the fresh fish are trucked to rivers like the Housatonic where anglers catch them and throw them back since they become so loaded with PCBs in the polluted water that the state health department recommends that no one eat more than one of these catches a month and not at all if one happens to be pregnant or young. This is a complicated and, to my mind, bizarre concept, but there you have it.

You can see all these little fishies from 8:00 A.M. to 3:30 P.M. seven days a week on Belden Road off Route 4 in Burlington. This is a short stop. I know—I had a twelve-year-old with me and she told me. For information, call 673–2340.

When you tire of the fishies or are told in clear terms that one of your party has tired of the fishies, head over to **Lamothe's Sugar House** (89 Stone Road) for a tour of their old-time maple sugar shed. It's open year-round from noon to 7:00 P.M. Monday through Thursday and noon to 5:00 P.M. Friday through Sunday. If you come on weekends from mid-February through the end of March, you can watch the Lamothes make the syrup. Their 2,200 maple trees drip sap into nearly 8 miles of tubing that leads to their gathering tanks. Watch them haul the tanks to the huge boiler in the sugarhouse, where the sap is turned to syrup and then to incredibly creamy candy, fudge, and taffy. Make sure you try "sugar on snow," based on a Vermont and French Canadian tradition of drizzling hot maple syrup over snow. The Lamothes use crushed ice to guarantee purity, and the result is the same—a gooey, gummy wonderful combination of ice and hardened syrup. The Lamothes also raise miniature lop-eared rabbits and golden retrievers, so a visit here also may include the chance to see some cute little creatures. For information, call 582–6135.

CANTON/COLLINSVILLE

Fishing and antiquing are probably the most popular tourist activities in the Canton/Collinsville area, but they are not likely to hold the attention of everyone in the family like **Huck Finn Adventures** will. Leisurely trips specially designed for families with young children or beginner canoeists are planned along a quiet section of the Farmington River between Avon and Simsbury. You choose from 3-, 5-, or 9-mile trips in flat water about waist-high over a sandy bottom. This outfitter provides everything you need for the outing except for the picnic or snacks you bring along. They set you up with stable 17-foot canoes, paddles, and lifevests. The charge per canoe is $40. Two adults and two young children are usually comfortable in one canoe. The trips are self-guided. Instruction is offered at the outset for novices, although this outing is gentle enough for little risk to true beginners. Perfect for folks with young children, the canoes have padded or canvas sling seats for the kids.

En route, you'll paddle past King Philip's Cave high up on the Talcott Mountain Ridge. You might want to stop near the old iron bridge along the way for a picnic at the Pinchot Sycamore, the largest tree in Connecticut. On the ride back to your put-in spot, the driver of your shuttle van will tell you the story of King Philip, or Metacomet, chief of the Wampanoags. A bloody three-year war began in 1675 when Metacomet began to massacre the settlers he feared would destroy his people. When Simsbury was burned by the Wampanoags in 1676, their notorious leader supposedly watched from the cave as the town went up in flames.

Two adults can do these trips in two to three hours (paddling time), but you're welcome to spend the day picnicking and exploring, or drifting like Huckleberry himself. Whitewater instruction is usually done in May and June as water conditions allow. For information, call 693–0385.

If you're intrigued by the history of the area after a day on the river, you might visit the **Canton Historical Society** at 11 Front Street. For information, call 693–2793. Canton also has a great wildlife sanctuary called **Roaring Brook Nature Center** (70 Gracey Road). An excellent longhouse typical of the Wampanoag people is part of its indoor exhibits. Six miles of trails through very pretty country are on the sanctuary grounds. Guided walks, concerts on summer Wednesday evenings, and a full complement of minicourses, workshops, and other events are offered. For information, call 693–0263.

EAST GRANBY

Amidst the beautiful hills of East Granby is a great family attraction—oddly enough, it's the **Old New-Gate Prison and Copper Mine** located on Newgate Road off Route 20. A National Historic Landmark, New-Gate was the first North American copper mine chartered by the British monarchy, in 1707. It was also Connecticut's first prison, named after London's notorious New-Gate Prison.

When copper mining ceased in the facility in 1773, due partly to the expense and danger of shipping the ore to England, the subterranean tunnels and chambers were deemed a perfect place to confine the burglars, horse thieves, and counterfeiters who had broken the laws of the English colonies. Soon, however, English sympathizers were imprisoned here as the American Patriots revolted against the monarchy and took New-Gate as their own. During the Revolutionary War, George Washington sent captured Tories here along with American deserters. Prisoners were forced to mine the tunnels until that enterprise, too, became unprofitable, even for use in the colonies. Just to make sure no one was having any fun underground, prisoners thereafter were forced to make nails and shoes.

The old brick rooms and ruins of the prison and much of the mine are now open to the public. A self-guided tour of the 65-foot-deep mine takes about thirty minutes. There is no handicapped access, and visitors should wear rubber soles for walking in the uneven and slippery rock tunnels. It's cool underground, too, so bring a sweatshirt.

I recommend *highly* that you call ahead and ask for a guided tour. Although all the guides are wonderfully educated as to the facts and fictions of this remarkable site, Mr. Chris Reilly is an extraordinary man and tour guide without peer. A veritable library of folklore, legend, history, humor, and outrageous opinion, he is a treasure himself. Ask for him.

The view from the prison grounds is one of the finest in the state; in particular, the fall foliage is glorious. You can picnic on the lawn or on tables. A great nature trail designed to demonstrate wildlife habitat management practices that homeowners can use on their own property is accessible from the parking lot. Pick up a guide to the trail inside the prison.

Old New-Gate is open from mid-May through October, Wednesday through Sunday, from 10:00 A.M. to 4:30 P.M. Adult admission is $3.00; children six to seventeen are $1.50, children under six are free. For information, call 566–3005 or 653–3563.

EAST WINDSOR

Follow Route 20 East from East Granby and pick up Route 140 East to get to the **Connecticut Trolley Museum.** If the kids are fans of *Mister Rogers Neighborhood,* they may enjoy a ride on one of the real live trolleys that make 3-mile excursions through the East Windsor woodlands. The museum owns nearly sixty trolleys from all over the world, but most of these sit on the side of the tracks waiting for restoration. Of the approximately ten that have been restored, two to eight may be out on the tracks on any given day. The open or closed cars run every fifteen minutes; your admission ticket buys you unlimited rides and a tour of the visitors center, which houses several restored cars, a steam locomotive, and a large model trolley collection. We rode a 1941 wooden car with wicker walkover seats from Hartford and a 1929 city car from Montreal.

The last two weekends in October feature two Halloween festivals. One is especially for children ages three to ten and features games, treats, prizes, and rides from 1:00 to 4:30 P.M. Later in the day, from 6:30 to 11:00 P.M. Fridays and Saturdays and Sundays from 6:30 to 9:30 P.M., children and adults can ride "Rails to the Darkside." The museum strongly suggests parental guidance for any child under thirteen. Ghouls of all kinds inhabit the woodlands—prepare for some frightening simulated mayhem. In December, the Winterfest features decorated cars and a canopy of colorful lights along the track through the woods.

Open daily from Memorial Day through Labor Day and Saturdays,

Sundays, and holidays from early September to late May. Hours from Memorial Day to Labor Day are 10:00 A.M. to 4:00 P.M. Monday through Friday, 10:00 A.M. to 6:00 P.M. Saturday, and noon to 6:00 P.M. Sunday. The rest of the year, the museum is open weekends only from noon to 5:00 P.M. Also open on weekday evenings during the Winterfest Light Display from December 1 through 23. Closed Thanksgiving Day, Christmas Eve, and Christmas Day. Adult admission is $6.00; children five to twelve are $3.00; and children under five are free. Festival admissions are $1.00–$2.00 more per ticket. For information, call 627–6540.

On the same property is the **Connecticut Fire Museum,** housing an amazing collection of vintage firefighting vehicles and equipment. An original 1904 switchboard alarm system, which still operates, is preserved exactly as it would have been used in decades past. The main hall contains twenty-one fire trucks, from a turn-of-the-century horse-drawn sleigh to a 1955 Zabek pumper. Other memorabilia, tools, and model fire trucks are also displayed. This museum is crowded and quite grimy, but if you love fire engines, this is the place to come. You can buy fire hats in the gift shop.

Open in April, May, September, and October on weekends only from noon to 5:00 P.M. and in June, July, and August from 10:00 A.M. to 4:00 P.M. Monday through Friday, 10:00 A.M. to 5:00 P.M. Saturday, and noon to 6:00 P.M. Sunday. Adults pay $2.00; children five to twelve pay $1.00, and children under five are free.

HARTFORD

The hub of the county is, of course, the state's capital city of Hartford. If you haven't been to the city with the family, plan to go soon. Like Connecticut's largest city, Bridgeport, Connecticut's oldest city, Hartford, holds a wealth of attractions suitable for the whole family. Founded in 1636 by Thomas Hooker and his Puritan followers, Hartford evolved from a peaceful agrarian community to a bustling industrial metropolis by 1900.

Hartford's neighborhoods grew more diverse with each wave of immigrants, and the people within the city limits invested their talents and energy in building a city of "firsts." Bushnell Park was the first public park in the United States to be conceived, built, and paid for by its citizens through popular vote. Elizabeth Park Rose Garden was the first municipal rose garden in the country. The Wadsworth Atheneum was the nation's first public art museum. These and many other important fixtures of the city provide ample incentive to explore Hartford time and time again.

For reasons of space alone, this volume will bring to your attention only a few highlights of Hartford. Many other worthwhile attractions exist. A call or visit to the Greater Hartford Tourism District at the Hartford Civic Center Information Desk at One Civic Center Plaza will help you obtain a pile several inches thick of brochures, maps, and guides. The Tourism District's telephone number is 520–4480 or (800) 793–4480.

For many years tourists have begun tours of Hartford at the **Old State House,** downtown at 800 Main Street. Having recently undergone a complete restoration, the state house is the perfect place in which families can orient themselves to the city and gain some perspective on its history. Built in 1796, on the site of the founding of the colony in 1636 by Hooker, the building is the oldest state house in the nation, established in service of the American people and their new Constitution.

The site on which George Washington greeted French General Rochambeau in 1780 when he arrived to assist the Patriot cause, the halls of the Old State House have also echoed with the footsteps of the Marquis de Lafayette, Andrew Jackson, and many other principal players of American history. But if you are thinking that this must be, therefore, a dusty, stodgy relic that expects quiet awe from whispering students on class trips, you're making a terrible mistake.

Along with its restoration, the Old State House has a whole new shtick. First of all, it's free—365 days a year. It's also 100 percent handicapped accessible, which is good news for those who ride in wheelchairs or strollers. With public restrooms, telephones, and signage in five languages plus Braille, the building is sparkling and airy in spite of its hallowed halls reputation. It invites—yes—*invites* children to touch, to run, to cheer, to ask questions. Costumed guides in character bring history to life on every floor. The kids won't realize they're being taught until they surprise themselves by telling you all they've learned.

In addition to concert and lecture halls and gallery exhibits of art and history, a visitor's center directs you to the city's best places. Bring a sturdy canvas bag if you want to add to your supply of brochures. On the second floor is Steward's Museum, a re-creation of the state's first museum founded by Joseph Steward, collector of everything extraordinary, impossible, and downright fraudulent. A smorgasbord of delights Barnumesque in nature the museum has among its wonders a unicorn's horn, an elephant's molar, a whole Bengal tiger, and an ostrich egg, just to name a few. All of these can be touched by children (and adults who behave appropriately).

The Old State House is open year-round Monday through Saturday from 10:00 A.M. to 5:00 P.M. and Sunday from noon to 5:00 P.M. Arrive ten minutes before 10:00 Monday through Saturday or at ten before noon Sunday to watch the staff fire the cannon on the front lawn. This place is one of the best small museums in the region. Call 522–6766.

Just 2 blocks from the Old State House at 600 Main Street is the **Wadsworth Atheneum,** a midsized museum housing works from ancient to modern times. The nation's oldest continuously operating public art museum, the Atheneum has a well-deserved reputation as one of the finest museums in the United States. Nineteenth-century Impressionist masters, major works from the Hudson River School, American and European decorative arts, a costume and textile gallery, several rooms from important architectural periods, the Armistad collection of African-American art, a gallery of contemporary art, and much more are here.

The museum offers a wonderful service to children—ask the folks at the main desk for "art cards," an incredible tool for making the museum appealing to kids. Each of the fifteen or more colorful cards has a game, a search, or an idea for exploring the galleries with children.

The museum's cafeteria has a children's menu, the exceptionally good gift shop is a place in which you could do all your holiday shopping, and the calendar of events includes an impressive array of films, workshops, concerts, and tours for families. For as long as support funds last, Shawmut Bank is sponsoring special family events each first Thursday of the month at no charge. Our girls and about one hundred other children created marvelous masks at an arts workshop that provided all supplies, while I enjoyed the artistry of a jazz combo playing in the courtyard. Special gallery tours directed to families are also offered on those days. Call the number below to be sure the program has continued.

The Wadsworth also offers a series of Sunday afternoon programs called Family Sundaes. Art activities, a theater program, and ice cream are part of the fun, which is held monthly during the academic year. Tickets must be purchased for Family Sundaes.

Open year-round with the exception of Mondays and major holidays, the museum hours are 11:00 A.M. to 5:00 P.M. Tuesday through Sunday. Children under thirteen are admitted at no charge at all times. Students thirteen and up pay $2.00, and adults pay $5.00, except all day Thursday and Saturday from 11:00 A.M. to 1:00 P.M. when admission for everyone is free. For information, call 278–2670.

From the museum, head west toward **Bushnell Park,** passing under Soldiers and Sailors Memorial Arch on Jewell Street at the entrance to the park. Dedicated to the 4,000 Hartford citizens who served in the Civil War, this huge sandstone arch depicts scenes from the war on its terra-cotta frieze. Look directly to your left immediately after passing through the arch and you'll find the **Bushnell Park Carousel** in a low, brown pavilion with beautiful stained-glass windows encircling its upper walls.

The completely restored 1914 carousel was hand-carved by master craftsmen Stein and Goldstein; its band organ is a 1924 Wurlitzer. Beautiful murals, lit by 800 lights, portray the seasons of the year. Forty-eight prancing horses on gleaming brass poles provide the best carousel ride we have had in the state. Compared to other carousels we have ridden, this carousel is *fast.* Parents, hold on to toddlers and don't be fooled by the slower warm-up of the first pass. You'll pay 50 cents per ride. Bring a pocketful of change—you'll ride this one more than once. Open mid-April to mid-May and in September on weekends only from 11:00 A.M. to 5:00 P.M. Also open from mid-May through August Tuesday through Sunday from 11:00 A.M. to 5:00 P.M. Birthday parties can be arranged. If you're in the city on December 31, come for the carousel's First Night celebration, a great way to hail the New Year. You might also enjoy the Haunted Carousel festivities in late October. Call 236–7739 or 249–2201.

When you escape the enchanting music of the Wurlitzer, you might notice the gleaming gold dome of the **State Capitol** building high on the hill to the right (or west) of the carousel. You can't miss it, actually. It's the icing on a rather overstated piece of cake, so to speak. Words like "monstrosity" have been used to describe this remarkable structure, but I believe most families will not be offended by its departures from architectural purism. To a child, this behemoth is just grand.

Tours of the Capitol and the Legislative Office Building connected to it are offered weekdays from September to June on the quarter-hours between 9:15 A.M. and 1:15 P.M. and Saturdays from April through October between 10:15 A.M. and 2:15 P.M. You can also stroll here yourselves. Pick up a self-guided tour brochure from Room 101. The tour includes visits to the public galleries of the assembly rooms, explanations of the functions of major offices, and information on how a bill becomes law.

If you are touring on your own, your first stop might be the main rotunda, where you can look up at the magnificent dome. The first floor also includes several pieces of sculpture—some huge, some graceful, like one of young Nathan Hale. A collection of Civil War memorabilia in the west wing is impressive; it includes uniforms, U.S. flags, and the equipment of important personages. My children were even more impressed by the nearby automated wooden Gothic doors that demanded several minutes of "Open, Sesame" shenanigans. Nothing like a little cultural edification. We also looked around quite a bit for the Governor: One of the girls had a complaint about mandatory elementary education. There's lots more here to see and do. The girls recommend walking backward on the people-mover in the tunnel between the Capitol and the LOB. Also, the girls would like you to know that you should definitely run and talk loudly because the whole place echoes. For information, call 240–0222.

Moving out of downtown, you might stop at **Elizabeth Park Rose Gardens** at Prospect and Asylum avenues. The first municipal rose garden in the country, this beautiful park has 15,000 rose bushes of 800 varieties. With lanes, arbors, and gazebos that bring *The Secret Garden* to mind, the formal garden is most glorious in late spring and throughout summer. Elizabeth Park's rock gardens, perennial and herb beds, and a trail through its forest of specimen trees make it a lovely spot to play. Truly a haven within the city, the park is especially therapeutic when music is playing, as it often is. A folk and bluegrass festival in August, a classical series on some Thursday evenings, jazz concerts sporadically, country dancing every Friday night in summertime, and special concerts for children are part of the Park's regimen for spiritual and mental nourishment. A children's story-hour at 10:00 A.M. Wednesdays in July and August features original and folk tales of a "green" theme told by professional storytellers, and free guided tours suitable for all ages take you through all or parts of the garden. On Father's Day come to the park's gala opening day of peak rose season. Called Rose Sunday, the event features music, food, art, tours, and activities for the whole family.

The Park extends across Prospect Avenue to acres of athletic fields and a children's play area with swings, tennis courts, and a picnic grove. The Elizabeth Park Overlook provides a panoramic view of the city as well as a gorgeous spot for watching the sunrise. Frisbee players, kite flyers, joggers, bicyclers, and lots of brides and grooms regularly inhabit this space in spring, summer, and fall. In winter you can sled on the huge hill near the overlook or skate (conditions permitting) on the pond. All this is possible, dawn to dusk, free of charge. For information, call 523–4276 or 722–6940.

Nook Farm (at the intersection of Farmington Avenue and Forest Street) is next on a must-do tour of Hartford. The site of a once-lively community of artists, writers, and other literate folk, it is most famed as the site of the homes of Mark Twain and Harriet Beecher Stowe. Quite bucolic in the nineteenth century, Nook Farm is now nearly eclipsed by Hartford and its suburb of West Hartford. Nevertheless, the homes and grounds give visitors a sense of the area's former air of gentility and simplicity.

Of course, simplicity is nowhere to be found in the home of novelist Samuel Langhorne Clemens, who gained fame as Mark Twain. The Gilded Age with all its splendid cacophony of detail is apparent in every inch of this remarkable home. Guided tours of the **Mark Twain House** are among the most excellent tours we have taken in the state. You will hear marvelous tales of the family's life and a generous sampling of the sardonic wit and wisdom of its owner.

The nineteen rooms of the house are beautifully restored to reflect its appearance in 1881, when the house was redecorated by a guild of artisans including Louis Comfort Tiffany. The tour includes all the family living quarters, Twain's private study where he did much of his writing, and the grounds surrounding the mansion. Twain's magnificent bed is a treasure in itself—Mrs. Clemens allowed the girls to remove the wooden angels from its posts and take them into the tub at bathtime!

The house is open year-round Tuesdays through Saturdays from 9:30 A.M. to 5:00 P.M. and Sundays from noon to 5:00 P.M. From June 1 through Columbus Day and in December, the house is also open on Mondays from 9:30 A.M. to 5:00 P.M. It is closed January 1, Easter Sunday, Labor Day, Thanksgiving, and December 24 and 25. Admission for adults is $6.50, and children six through sixteen pay $2.75. The last tour begins shortly before 4:00 P.M. daily. For information, call 247–0998.

Just across the lawn at 71 Forest Street is the **Harriet Beecher Stowe House,** built in 1871 as a cottage for Mrs. Stowe and her family. The house is austere compared to the gaudy character of the Twain House, but it is in itself a serenely beautiful Victorian dwelling that has been restored in every detail. The last residence of Harriet Beecher Stowe, whose *Uncle Tom's Cabin* can be said to have changed the course of U.S. history, this house, like Twain's, is furnished mostly with items belonging to the Stowe family. My favorite room is the kitchen, which is patterned closely after the model kitchen described by Stowe and her sister Catherine in their book, *The American Woman's Home.*

Though the Stowe House tours are somewhat drier in nature than the Twain tours, docents here make many attempts to tailor their talks to the interests of any children present. The house is filled with many decorative arts done by Stowe herself. An accomplished painter, she often painted the flowers she loved to grow in her gardens. Outside, the gardens have been replanted with the many exotic and native perennials that Stowe grew here before her death in 1896.

Tours of the Stowe House include a trip to her niece's house on the corner of the Nook Farm property at Farmington Avenue and Forest Street. The Katherine Seymour Day House contains personal belongings of Harriet Beecher Stowe and excellent historical exhibits that explain the effect *Uncle Tom's Cabin* had on the abolitionist movement and the Civil War. It also includes exhibits on nineteenth-century architecture, decorative arts, history, and literature. A research library on these subjects as well as social reform, women's suffrage, and women's studies in general is open by appointment. Children are welcome to use the library. A letter of recommendation from a teacher or librarian is necessary to gain access.

The Stowe House is open on the same schedule as the Twain House;

the last tour of each day begins shortly before 4:00 P.M. Tickets are purchased in the Carriage House Visitors Center, which houses an introductory exhibit on the Beecher family as well as a gift shop. Adult admission costs $6.00; children six to sixteen pay $2.75. Stowe House hosts several events designed especially for children. A free summer concert series, a Halloween festivity, a Christmas tour, and a celebration of Mrs. Stowe's birthday are among the activities. For information, call 525–9317.

KENSINGTON

In the village of Kensington, southeast of the city of New Britain, you will find the **Hungerford Outdoor Education Center** at 191 Farmington Avenue, which is Route 372. Part Two, so to speak, of the New Britain Youth Museum (see page 72), the Hungerford Center consists of twenty-seven acres of forest, swamp, pond, and wetland habitats. Actively involved in local outreach programs that are initiated through schools and youth organizations, the center is also open to visitors of the daytripping variety.

Exhibits on natural history, geology, and agriculture are the indoor features of the center's Cooper Hall. Its theme, "Domestication of the Earth," explains the processes by which humans have tamed the land, animals, and plants of Connecticut to provide themselves with shelter, food, and clothing. Built in a restored 1920s show-horse stable, separate "stalls" of the exhibit area deal with such subjects as plants and people, farm tools, and solar energy. A pig, goat, cow, and chickens are among the animals in the Hungerford Barnyard, and native wildlife, some exotic animals, and an injured wildlife rehab compound are also here.

Outside the Nutrition Kitchen is a cottage garden of medicinal and culinary herbs. Along with this are raised beds of organically fertilized fruits, vegetables, and perennials planted as demonstration gardens. You may bring home some great ideas from this place. A trail system and a pond with observation stations are all part of the complex. Picnic tables (but no trash containers) are provided. You can't feed the animals yourselves, but you are welcome to leave fresh fruit or vegetables as a donation.

The trails are open from dawn to dusk; you can hike here free of charge. Live animal programs are presented Saturday at 11:00 A.M. and 1:00 and 3:00 P.M. year-round. Given in Cooper Hall, they are open to those who have paid admission to that part of the center. Cooper Hall admission is $2.00 for adults, $1.00 for children two to seventeen, and free to those under two. Open year-round Tuesday through Friday from 1:00 to 5:00 P.M. and Saturday from 10:00 A.M. to 5:00 P.M. In the summer, the center is open Tuesday through Saturday from 10:00 A.M. to 5:00 P.M. Closed Sundays, Mondays, and holidays, Hungerford Center offers a wide variety of family programs open to members and visitors. Some are intended for children only; others are events for the whole family. Recent programs have included a summer solstice stroll and a marine magic ocean life study. For information, call 827–9064.

NEW BRITAIN

Southeast of Hartford is the small city of New Britain, a city with a past characterized by the dubious distinction of the nickname "Hardware City" and an ethnic population that included every major European nation and most of the minor ones. The steady pace at the tool works has slowed in recent years, and the immigrant groups have mixed and changed, but the city is much the same—a modest metropolis with a low-key reputation that usually keeps it well out of the limelight. New Britain has some buried treasures, though. You'll want to spend at least a day here discovering some of its secrets.

Your first stop might be the **New Britain Youth Museum** at 30 High Street. Placing this facility in a book like this one is a real judgment call, and I'll tell you why: The New Britain Youth Museum is not new, it's not big, it's not slick or sleek or sophisticated. Some days it's downright sleepy, and on most days there are only a few activities going on. You may not spend more than an hour here, and you might even be annoyed if you drive an hour to get here and discover it has only two rooms of exhibits. Here's the dilemma: All that considered, this place is terrific for kids. At this little wonder last summer, we viewed two of the best exhibitions we've seen anywhere. We also participated in one of the best, and least expensive, children's workshops we've ever done. It's our understanding that shows and workshops of this caliber are common here.

The museum has an extensive permanent collection of natural history specimens, dolls, toys, and circus memorabilia and a continuing focus on historical and cultural artifacts of childhood. Curator Deborah Pfeiffenberger has a special touch for changing exhibitions and is committed to creating excellent multilevel, multicurricular, and interactive signage for each exhibit. Recent exhibits included the *Dolls of Japan: Shapes of Prayer, Embodiments of Love* and *Folk Dolls: Sticks and Stones, Rags and Bones.* Comprised of dolls both on loan and in the museum's collection, the folk doll exhibition, for example, was outstanding—the finest collection of folk dolls I have ever seen in one place with the *best* signage directed to young audiences that I have ever read. Our girls made straw folk dolls in a workshop that lasted fifty minutes, cost fifty cents, and supplied everything they needed to go home with their own folk toy, *and* included a mini-lecture and discussion of folk art.

Pfeiffenberger's love of art and children's literature has also prompted many exhibitions celebrating the works of famed illustrators of children's books. These exhibitions are usually on loan and change somewhat frequently. The museum has a terrific puppet theater area and a small, rather worn outdoor play area. Much of the museum's work is with schools and local youth organizations, but if you're planning to be in New Britain, our experience would indicate that a stop here would be worthwhile. Call the number below and ask for information on the current programs and exhibits. See page 71 for information on the museum's outdoor exhibits at the Hungerford Center in Kensington.

The New Britain facility is open September through June Tuesday through Friday from 1:00 to 5:00 P.M. and Saturday from 10:00 A.M. to 4:00 P.M. In summer, it opens at 11:00 A.M. Tuesday through Friday and is closed on Saturdays. For information, call 325–3020.

Head next to the **New Britain Museum of American Art** at 56 Lexington Street. This attraction poses no dilemma at all. Perfect for young families because of its very manageable size, it is in every way a gem of an art museum. Housed in a beautiful turn-of-the-century mansion built by William Hart, founder of New Britain's Stanley Works tool company, the museum has an unusually welcoming ambience and excellent tour materials with which you can gain a full understanding of the outstanding art collected here. A poster perched on an easel in the foyer captures the essence of the museum's philosophy: WHENEVER YOU VISIT THE NEW BRITAIN

MUSEUM OF AMERICAN ART, WE WANT YOU TO FEEL FREE TO LAUGH, TALK, TAKE THE KIDS, HOLD HANDS, ASK QUESTIONS, VOICE AN OPINION, GAWK, EXPRESS YOUR-SELF, LEARN SOMETHING NEW, STAY AS LONG AS YOU LIKE, COME BACK AGAIN.

Visitors are invited to touch the woodwork and sit in the furniture, and the tour book adds, "By the way, do not feel anxious if your children are a bit noisy or active. We are delighted to have visitors of all ages." In fact, they have created an exceptionally good tour book called *Looking at Art* just for children.

The museum's 5,000 holdings from the early eighteenth century to the present are supplemented by a gallery for changing exhibitions of works on loan, although if you were only to see the permanent collection you still would be viewing some of the greatest treasures of American art. Gilbert Stuart, Asher Durand, Thomas Cole, Frederic Church, Winslow Homer, Maxfield Parrish, John Singer Sargent, Mary Cassatt, Childe Hassam, Georgia O'Keefe, N. C. Wyeth, Andrew Wyeth, Norman Rockwell, and Thomas Hart Benton are just some of the artists represent-ed here. *The Arts of Life in America* murals in the Thomas Hart Benton Gallery are stunning. Children and adults alike are transfixed by their mag-

The New Britain Museum of American Art is a great place to introduce your kids to the wonder of art. (Courtesy New Britain Museum of Art)

nificence. The sculptures of Solon Borglum are also compelling representations of Native Americans and the American West.

If you have never taken your children to an art museum, begin here. The museum is open year-round Tuesday through Sunday from 1:00 to 5:00 P.M. Closed Mondays and holidays. Admission is free. For information, call 229–0257.

By the way, the museum overlooks **Walnut Hill Park,** designed by Frederick Law Olmsted, who was also the landscape architect of New York City's Central Park. Walnut Hill Park's sweeping lawns and towering oak trees make it a perfect place to play or picnic.

ROCKY HILL

If your children have been drawn into the dinosaur mania of the last decade or so, they'll love Rocky Hill's **Dinosaur State Park.** The area called "Rockie Hill" in colonial days was far different 185 million years ago. Then it was a bona fide Jurassic Park—a wide mud flat on the edge of a broad, shallow lake that filled a basin carved by glaciers a few million years before that. The lake was densely populated with vegetation, fish, and small reptiles of a roughly crocodilian description. The dinosaurs roaming nearby liked the menu, so they stayed until their luck ran out in the next ecological disaster.

Now only their tracks remain, a fact discovered during excavations in the 1960s for a modern ecological disaster called an office building. Bulldozer operator Ed McCarthy noticed something unusual about the ground he was clearing, and soon the place was crawling with paleontologists. Many of the 2,000 tracks uncovered have been re-covered to preserve them, but about 500 are exposed to public view. A giant geodesic dome protects the mostly three-toed impressions from the elements. A walkway around the tracks provides a good view, and a full-scale reproduction of the sort of dinosaur most likely to have made the tracks stands in a running pose on the platform above the pit.

Visitors are invited to make plaster casts of some of the tracks. Signs provide the instructions, but you must provide the quarter-cup of vegetable oil and the ten pounds of plaster of Paris necessary to complete the project. If you decide to do this, you have to be finished by 3:30 P.M. The park also has a dinosaur bookstore, forty acres of nature preserve with hiking trails, and a picnic area.

The outdoor areas are open daily year-round (except on major holidays) from 9:00 A.M. to 4:30 P.M. Fair warning: Call before you visit if you are planning a trip in 1995. The Exhibit Center under the dome is currently closed for repairs and improvements, with a projected reopening of Fall 1995. Outside the dome there is no evidence of prehistoric life, and we don't want you to be disappointed. The park charges no admission fee; before it closed for renovation, the Exhibit Center charged $2.00 for adults and $1.00 for children six through seventeen. Children under six are free. For information, call 529–8423.

SIMSBURY

Simsbury is an appealing suburb of 23,000 people, many of whom work in Hartford, just twenty minutes southeast. Established in 1670 by English colonists, Simsbury was built on land long populated by the Wampanoag Indians, who had no understanding of the English concept of land claims when they began to share their tribal lands with the newcomers. Their misapprehension of the situation led to some turbulence that culminated in the burning of Simsbury by the Indians on March 26, 1676. Sad to say, the Wampanoag people underestimated the tenacity of the settlers and were nearly eradicated in the bloody King Philip's war that ensued. Reconstruction of colonial Simsbury commenced in 1677 when it was clear that no further resistance was possible. The settlers of Simsbury soon had a thriving community that flourished over the next several centuries along with its industries of copper mining, smelting, steel production, copper coinage, silver plating, and safety fuse manufacturing. Now largely residential, Simsbury offers to the public one of the best historical settlements in the state.

Called **Massacoh Plantation,** the settlement is in the center of Simsbury at 800 Hopmeadow Street. The "plantation" has eight structures—some reproductions, some original to the property, and some transported here for the purpose of creating the museum.

A tour of the property usually begins at the 1683 meetinghouse where the Simsbury founding fathers decided matters of both church and

state and from which supposed witch Goody Griffin is said to have depart-
ed by flying through its keyhole. The building is a reproduction. The 1771
Elisha Phelps House was occupied by the Phelps family for nearly 200
years. It is restored to the period of the 1830s when it served as a
hotel/tavern for travelers on the New Haven–Northampton Canal. The
site also includes a Victorian carriage house with an authentic tin peddler's
cart, a 1740 one-room schoolhouse, a barn, an icehouse, a 1795 cottage
also owned by the Phelps family, and a re-creation of the safety fuse man-
ufactory with fixtures, records, and furnishings of the original plant.

Tours by (usually) costumed docents are thorough and excellent,
though a full tour for children under age eight may be longer than they can
bear. You can stroll the grounds unguided, but you cannot tour the buildings without a docent. You might want to bring the children to the
Massacoh Plantation's holiday festivity in late November or early
December. Called "Three Centuries by Candlelight," this special tour is a
fully costumed living-history reenactment of a series of scenes from
Simsbury's past. Like Charles Dickens's Scrooge, you watch the scenes
unfold as the actors go about their drama as though you were not there.
All this happens by candlelight, of course, since the houses are not electri-
fied. This is a very impressive event, marvelous for children and adults.

Massacoh Plantation is open May through October, Sunday through
Friday from 1:00 to 4:00 P.M. and Saturday by appointment. The last full
tour begins at 3:00 P.M. Adult admission is $5.00; children are charged
$2.50. Tickets for the holiday reenactment are extra. For information, call
658–2500.

If the excellent history lessons at Massacoh Plantation overwhelm
some in your party, you might refresh yourselves with a brisk hike at
Talcott Mountain State Park. A popular family hiking area because of
the amazing Heublein Tower at the summit of Talcott Mountain Ridge, the
park offers moderate trails, benches, picnic sites, and, on clear days, views
of four states from the tower. The park overlooks many of the fertile
Farmington Valley farms and pretty towns like Avon. From Route 10
between Simsbury and Avon, you can't miss seeing the white 165-foot-tall
tower built in 1914 by businessman Gilbert Heublein.

Once you're in the park, which you reach from Route 185, you hike the 1.25-mile King Philip's Trail to the tower and then climb up the tower, if you can manage the stairs. The park itself is open year-round from dawn to dusk. Heublein Tower is open Thursday through Sunday from 10:00 A.M. to 5:00 p.m., April 1 through Labor Day and daily from 10:00 A.M. to 5:00 P.M. Labor Day through October to accommodate all the foliage lovers. For information, call 566–2304.

SOUTHINGTON

The town of Southington lies halfway between New York and Boston just east of I–84, a location that even in pre-highway days helped it become an important industrial community, producing cement, tinware, and carriage hardware in the nineteenth century and aircraft parts, electronic equipment, and medical instruments in the twentieth. With all the work folks do in these parts, there needs to be a time and place for play. Southington offers both.

For a week every October, Southington's population swells by many thousands as the annual **Apple Harvest Festival** attracts an estimated 300,000 revelers. For more than a quarter of a century, this festival has celebrated the Southington apple crop in every way possible—a parade, a carnival, a road race, apple foods and ethnic foods, music, arts and crafts, dancing, and an all-around good time. Admission is free. Follow the crowds to the Town Green on Route 10. It's usually the first weekend in October, plus the following Thursday, Friday, Saturday, and Sunday. Saturday, the festival runs from 10:00 A.M. to 10:00 p.m.; Sunday it's noon to 8:00 p.m., and Thursday and Friday it's 5:30 to 10:00 P.M.

The festivities extend to the orchards themselves. Each of four orchards in Southington has a showroom full of apples, cider, candies, other produce, and gifts. You can also pick your own apples in the orchards. For directions to Roger's, Novick's, Doran's, or Lewis's farm and for information on the festival, call 628–8036.

Mount Southington Ski Area provides the place to play in Southington. If hiking in summer or skiing in winter appeals to your family, Mount Southington is a good place to start. Fourteen downhill trails with five surface lifts and two chair lifts provide ample space for young families who don't want to travel too far to ski. You can snow-board here, too, but cross-country skiers will have to go elsewhere. A snack bar and cafe, night skiing, a ski shop, rentals, and lessons are all part of the business here. More than one hundred professional instructors give group and private lessons, including the SKIWEE program for four- to twelve-year-olds. Who knows? Your future Olympic champion may start out on these slopes. Snow-making machines keep the slopes active from November through much of early spring. Come early to Mount Southington's annual Ski Swap in late October (usually the last weekend) for great deals on equipment for beginners and veterans. The area is located off exit 30 of I–84; after that, follow the signs to 396 Mt. Vernon Road. For information, call 628–0954.

WEST HARTFORD

West Hartford sashays outward from the left of Hartford just as smooth as Fred Astaire and with just as much debonair grace. It's one of Connecticut's more affluent communities and if you can dodge the Volvos making turns on Farmington Avenue and LaSalle Road, you'll find terrific shops and restaurants in its upscale downtown. All things considered, our family likes West Hartford. It's pretty, it's clean and safe, the food and shopping are well above average, and two people we love live here. It's a good place to spend a family weekend. You can take in the boutiques, visit the Noah Webster House, and spend some time at the Science Center of Connecticut.

If you start a West Hartford tour in the shops, make sure you stop at **Barker's Animation Art Gallery** at 60A LaSalle. You'll be dragging the kids out when it's time to leave, if you're not hooked yourself. They sell original cels here—the transparencies from animated films. Disney, Warner Brothers, Hanna-Barbera, and other famous animation artworks are sold along with related items like watches and jewelry. Original Disney storyboard pencil sketches are also sold here. The Winnie-the-Pooh drawings were our favorites. Enjoy! For information, call 232–TOON.

Just outside the main thoroughfare is the **Noah Webster House** at 227 South Main Street. The birthplace and childhood home of the author of the first American dictionary, Noah Webster House is one of the best colonial restorations in the state, not least of all because it was the home of one of America's finest citizens. An excellent short film introduces visitors to Webster's story and the history of the house, and guided tours by costumed docents fill in the gaps of the tale. Our girls enjoy these tales because their own home was built in 1740 and they can usually identify artifacts and architectural features as well as the docents can. Here, they were outsmarted—the docents had much to teach them.

The house has a very active calendar of family and children's events—genealogy workshops, open hearth cooking, kitchen herb classes, colonial dancing and games, and much more. Children going into grades four, five, and six can participate in the Colonial Child Summer Camp, a week of activities typical of an eighteenth-century childhood.

Even if you come only for the day, you'll see Noah Webster's desk and clocks and 200 original editions of his books, including his *Blue-Backed Speller* and the 1828 dictionary referred to in the introduction of this book (and which he spent nearly twenty-seven years writing). The house is open for tours October 1 to June 14, Thursday through Tuesday from 1:00 to 4:00 p.m., and June 15 to September 30, Monday, Tuesday, Thursday, and Friday from 10:00 A.M. to 4:00 P.M. and Saturday and Sunday from 1:00 to 4:00 P.M. Admission for adults is $3.00; children six through fifteen pay $1.00. For information, call 521–5362.

The **Science Center of Connecticut** (950 Trout Brook Drive) is currently one of the best science and technology museums in the state, but huge strides are being undertaken to make it one of the best in the nation. A work-in-progress for the next few years, the new facility will have at its heart the Science Center's philosophy that scientific principles are best learned through experience as well as explanation. Current and future exhibits are and will be interactive, allowing children and adults to discover scientific facts and to conduct experiments that reinforce those findings.

Even now, the Science Center offers excellent opportunities for learning. The live animal center has a diverse collection of birds, reptiles, and mammals from around the world. Live animal demonstrations are given daily. In the IBM Computer Center, visitors use computers to control mechanized LEGO machines among many other programs. In the Discovery Room, young visitors can explore concepts of light, color, water, and communications. The Long Island Sound Touch-Tank offers a chance to learn about marine ecology, and the outdoor Paleo-Pit simulates an archeological dig. The world's largest walk-in kaleidoscope, a model of the

Hubble Space telescope, and an outdoor full-scale walk-in model of Connecticut's state animal, the sperm whale, are all part of the current museum.

In addition, the main exhibition hall features major changing exhibitions. We recently saw an outstanding robotics show, and an automated dinosaur show is among the upcoming exhibits. The Gengras Planetarium explores the sun, stars, and galaxy along with daily laser light shows. Evening laser shows feature rock, country, classical, and jazz programs. Many shows are accompanied by environmental or mythical narratives.

A wide array of workshops, camp programs, research projects, and activity-based science and math courses are offered for individuals, families, and teachers through the Science Center.

The facility is open year-round, Tuesday through Saturday from 10:00 A.M. to 5:00 P.M. and Sunday from noon to 5:00 P.M. It is also open summer and holiday Mondays from 10:00 A.M. to 5:00 p.m., but it is closed on major holidays. General admission for adults is $5.00; children five through fifteen pay $4.00; children under four are free. Planetarium and laser shows are an additional charge, which varies according to the program. For information, call 236–2961.

WETHERSFIELD

The historical center of Wethersfield is in itself a miniature living-history museum, the largest authentic historic district in the state. Its pretty Main and Broad streets are chock-full of beautifully restored seventeenth- and eighteenth-century homes that reflect Wethersfield's history as the first permanent settlement in the Colony and the most northerly trading post on the Connecticut River. I recommend that history buffs spend a day here. It is easy to enjoy the fantasy that one has stepped back in time in Wethersfield. Here are the high points of a town tour:

The Wethersfield Historical Society, based at 150 Main Street, is comprised of three buildings, including the 1793 Captain James Francis House at 120 Hartford Avenue, which traces a single family through 170 years. A library, archives, a museum shop, and exhibits on Wethersfield's history are housed in the other buildings. Tours and family programs are offered regularly throughout the year, except for the Francis House, which is open only mid-May through mid-October. Call 529–7656.

The **Webb–Deane–Stevens Museum** at 211 Main Street includes three eighteenth-century homes, each restored and furnished to provide a glimpse into distinct periods of American life. The houses, respectively, offer a look at the family lifestyles of a merchant, a diplomat, and a trades-man spanning the years from 1690 to 1840. The gardens behind the three houses are extraordinary, featuring flowers and herbs of the eighteenth century. Tours are offered every hour from May 1 to October 31 on Wednesday through Monday from 10:00 A.M. to 4:00 P.M. and from November 1 to April 30 Saturday and Sunday from 10:00 A.M. to 4:00 P.M. For information and rates, call 529–0612.

The 1700 **Buttolph–Williams House** at 249 Broad Street reflects the medieval architecture of a turn-of-the-eighteenth-century "mansion" house. Furnished to provide a sense of an affluent family within a Puritan community, the house is the site of many fine family events, workshops, and celebrations. Open only from May 15 to October 15 from noon to 4:00 p.m., Tuesday through Sunday. Adult admission is $2.00; children are $1.00. For information, call 247–8996.

Comstock, Ferre and Company at 263 Main Street is the oldest continuously operating seed company in the United States. A nationally known concern since 1840, it still sells seeds, plants, crafts, and gifts from its eighteenth-century post-and-beam warehouses. This is a great place for kids to explore. Take home some of their wonderful heirloom seeds or bulbs for your own gardens. Open Tuesday through Saturday from 9:00 A.M. to 5:30 P.M. For information, call 529–3319.

WINDSOR LOCKS

Right within sight of the runways at Bradley International Airport is the **New England Air Museum** (take Route 20 to Route 75 and follow the signs). The largest aviation history museum in the Northeast, it is one of only four such collections in the United States. From a 1909 wood and canvas Bleriot XI monoplane to modern jets, the museum includes seventy-five aircraft of military and civilian origins. Most are restored and housed inside two hangars, transformed to museum gallery quality.

Excellent exhibits tell the story of flight from the drawings of Leonardo da Vinci to the space flights of NASA astronauts. The evolution of humankind's mastery of gravity is chronicled at every turn, nowhere more clearly than in the aircraft themselves. The museum owns the oldest aeronautical artifact in the United States—a beautiful wicker balloon basket built by Silas Brooks of Plymouth, Connecticut, in 1870. From that vintage onward, the museum houses biplanes, Piper Cubs, Seabat helicopters, B-25 bombers, Grumman Hellcats and Wildcats, F-4 Phantom jets, hang-gliders, and many other fully and partially restored aircraft.

Charles Lindbergh memorabilia, an outstanding Igor Sikorsky exhibit, and an airmail display are among the special areas. The museum's theater presents continuous films on flight, the space program, military aircraft history, and other topics. Come on Open Cockpit Sundays (offered a few times annually) if you'd like to climb inside the cockpits of several of the restored aircraft. Most of the signage is directed to adults. Parents of young children will have to read and/or paraphrase most of the excellent information provided by the museum. Despite this problem, the museum is well-suited to children, and the museum shop is full of fun merchandise perfect for kids. The museum is open daily year-round, except Thanksgiving and Christmas, from 10:00 A.M. to 5:00 P.M. Admission for those between twelve and sixty is $6.00. Children six to eleven pay $3.00; those under six are free. For information, call 623–3305.

By the way, the road to the museum runs right alongside the airport runway. Pull over and sit there awhile for great views of the coming and goings of local, national, and international aircraft.

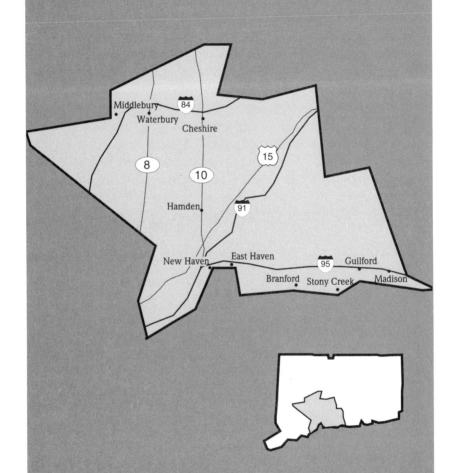

Middlebury

Waterbury

84

Cheshire

8

15

10

Hamden

91

New Haven

East Haven

95

Guilford

Branford

Stony Creek

Madison

New Haven County

NEW HAVEN COUNTY

Shaped loosely like a five-pointed star, this county reaches widely from its historic center in the city of New Haven. The small cities of Meriden and Waterbury in the north are balanced by suburban towns and rural villages to the east and west. Sliced into three parts by the Quinnipiac and Naugatuck rivers, the county is usually perceived more along those divisions than as a whole.

New Haven is most definitely the cultural center of the county. Like Hartford and Bridgeport, New Haven struggles to overcome the public perception that the city is a dangerous place. In fact, areas of interest to tourists are well cared for, well lit, and well protected. Both in and outside of its cities, New Haven County is a great place for adventurous families.

BRANFORD/STONY CREEK

What a pleasure to be able to begin New Haven County with the following tour. One of the prettiest and most relaxing family excursions in the state centers in and around Stony Creek, as quintessential a quaint New England fishing village as can be found in these parts. Only Stonington in New London County transports one more thoroughly to the nautical past.

Actually a part of the town of Branford, Stony Creek has a long and lively history, complete with tales of pirate treasure and other romances of the sea and heart. The village is now famed for its quiet Yankee charm and its sprinkling of pink granite islands just offshore—the Thimbles.

In fact, the village's principal industry, if one can call it that, is the **Thimble Islands** sightseeing tour business. Three enterprising captains have updated the centuries-old trade of ferrying livestock, groceries, visitors, and even the occasional piano from the town dock to the islands. Now, from mid-May through Columbus Day, landlubbers can board ship to enjoy the sea breeze and scenery while listening to the colorful tales of the islands' past and present.

From Captain Kidd to General Tom Thumb, the stories told by Captain Bob Milne aboard the *Volsunga III* are exceeded in quality only by his sure navigation of the reefs surrounding the twenty-three inhabited islands of the total 365. Milne's green and white wooden vessel is a converted Downeast lobster boat, rated for thirty-three passengers and the smallest of the three cruise options.

Captain Bob's easygoing manner makes for terrific storytelling, easily heard over the *Volsunga's* recently improved sound system and its sound-proofed engine. Along with views of the islands' ninety-five homes, which range from a palatial Spanish mansion to Victorian cottages to a veritable aerie on stilts, we enjoyed the sights of human and winged islanders—kids wearing life jackets while playing in their yards, teens diving from rocks, and cormorants, terns, herons, and gulls to spare.

The Volsunga III leaves the dock every hour on the hour, weather permitting, from 10:00 A.M. to 4:00 P.M. daily from July 1 until the day before Labor Day. From mid-May through June and from Labor Day through Columbus Day, the tour times differ somewhat, with fewer cruises given daily and no operation on Mondays of several weeks at either end of the season. Call Captain Bob at 488–9978 for reservations or 481–3345 for information.

For details on the similar schedules of the other cruises, call Captain Mike of the *Sea Mist II* at 488–8905 or Captain Dave at the *Sea Venture I* at 397–3921. Ticket prices for all cruises are $5.00 for adults and $3.00 for children under twelve. To reach the Stony Creek Dock, take I-95 to exit 56, and go south on Leetes Island Road for 2 miles. At the stop sign, go straight on Thimble Island Road, and follow the signs to the dock.

On your ride down to the water, you may notice Stony Creek's other attractions. The **Stony Creek Puppet House** is the site of a handful of theater and improvisation productions each summer and sporadically throughout the year. It is also home to the **Macri–Weil Sicilian Puppet Theater,** led by puppetmasters Jim Weil and Salvatore Macri.

The puppets themselves are extraordinary 4- to 5-foot-tall figures with heads of hand-carved walnut and bodies of wood and steel covered with hemp and canvas. Beautifully painted and dressed in armors of hand-embossed brass, these hundred-year veterans of the stage battle each other in enactments of tales of the Crusades, Charlemagne and his Paladins, and the Sicilian Knights. You'll be on the edge of your theater seat at these remarkable performances. Call 488–8511.

Stop next door to the theater for a look at **Black-Eyed Designs,** a tiny store with an eclectic and very funky collection of new and used goods. Down the street toward the dock is **Stony Creek Antiques** with a decidedly less plebian collection, the **Stony Creek Market** (great for soft drinks and picnic fare), and the **Stony Creek Marine and Tackle and Fish Market,** which also carries drinks, deli foods, and snacks. Stony Creek Market is the only sit-down place to eat in the village. Take the over-stuffed sandwiches, big enough for two small kids to share, out on the front deck for a great view of the harbor. From 5:00 to 9:00 P.M. Tuesday through Sunday, the Market doubles as **Stony Creek Pizza.**

If you really want to soak up the scenery here, leave the village and follow picturesque Route 146 to the west through Branford's other pretty enclaves of Pine Orchard and Indian Neck. If you drive by **Lenny's Indian Head Inn** (205 South Montowese Street) without turning in for dinner, you'll be missing their famed menu of New England seafood, epitomized in Lenny's Famous Shore Dinner of clam chowder, cherrystones, sweet corn on the cob, lobster, steamers, and watermelon. Steaks, burgers, fries and rings, homemade cole slaw, and a children's menu served in the ambience of worn wood floors and wooden booths make this a thumbs-up place for families.

CHESHIRE

Centered near Routes 10 and 70 toward the north of the county, Cheshire was founded in 1690 by families who made their living as farmers, a fact that still influences this suburb. Chesire is a bedroom community for New

Haven, Meriden, Hartford, and Waterbury, but it is also a region of nurseries, orchards, dairy farms, and vineyards.

Right on Route 70 is one of the oldest and best of these farms. **Bishop Farm** represents the work of five generations. In business since 1805, Bishop's grows and sells apples, peaches, pears, plums, blueberries, and raspberries. In the fall they make cider and apple juice at their mill—you can watch them do so on pressing days and then buy some to take home.

Recently, Bishop's has undergone a million-dollar renovation. It now has a gift shop and snack bar from which you can purchase Vermont cheese, pure honey, 100 percent natural ice cream, fresh chicken pot pies, apple crisp, gourmet coffees, and soft drinks. A Christmas shop is open in season, and Harvest House next door sells seasonal gifts and home accessories such as dried flowers, fresh wreaths, and other holiday treats.

Pony rides, hayrides, a petting barnyard, and pick-your-own fruits are part of the fun here. Last season 73,000 pounds of pumpkins left these fields. You are welcome to walk the trails through the orchards and relax near the pond while you have an apple cider doughnut made with cider instead of water.

Like other Connecticut farms, the need to survive economically has forced this business to diversify, so a vineyard and winery are also here. Christmas trees for are sale from Thanksgiving through December. Call for pick-your-own information and remember that the level of activity here varies with the weather and the seasons. If you intend to make this an outing in itself, call 272–8243 to see what's happening.

Cheshire has another pair of ambitious entrepreneurs who hope to bring pleasure to children. Herb and Gloria Barker, who own Barker's Animation Art Gallery in West Hartford, have opened the **Cartoon and Comic Art Museum** at 1188 Highland Avenue, which is Route 10. Located on converted farm property, this museum celebrates American animation and comic and cartoon art from the 1920s to the present.

The complex includes another of the Barkers' very successful art galleries, but it also features several components entirely for your entertainment. On weekends now and perhaps more often in the future, the outdoor Storybook Stage showcases life-sized costumed characters performing Disney versions of classic stories. Also outside, a re-creation of Snow

Kids will love a trip to the Cartoon and Comic Art Museum. (Photo by Herb Barker)

White's wishing well sings in response to your push of a button. Strolling characters greet visitors, and statuary of characters dot the landscape.

Inside, a cartoon theater plays classic cartoon movies from the 1930s, and in the museum area, thousands upon thousands of transparencies, comic strips, toys, trinkets, and other memorabilia of the art and industry of cartooning are displayed for your perusal. This is the place to learn the complete stories of Betty Boop, Raggedy Ann and Andy, Sylvester, and hundreds of other characters. You'll discover some of the fascinating details of the technology, art, and history of many classic films.

The museum is open year-round at no charge, Wednesday through Saturday from 9:30 A.M. to 5:30 P.M. and Sunday from noon to 5:00 P.M. For information and updated hours, call 272–2357.

Cheshire has joined other communities across the United States in reclaiming for recreational and historic preservation purposes the valuable land of abandoned rail lines and canal routes. Thus far, the town maintains a $2\frac{9}{10}$-mile section that ends at the Hamden town line. A $2\frac{9}{10}$-mile Hamden section will soon pick up where this one leaves off, and Cheshire awaits use of another section to be abandoned in the near future by the local railway.

Called the **Farmington Canal Linear Park,** this ribbon of land was once on the property of the Farmington Canal, built in 1828 and extending from New Haven Harbor to Northampton, Massachusetts. The longest canal in New England, it was eventually replaced by a railroad along the same corridor. Now a 12-foot-wide pathway has replaced the railway, and the picturesque canal flows beside it. Open dawn to dusk at no charge, the wooded pathway is used by joggers, walkers, rollerbladers, and cyclists year round, and in the winter, whenever there is snow, a swatch is left unplowed for cross-country skiers.

Many families use the park, and on some weekends they can stop at the park-within-the-park at Lock 12 of the canal for a tour of the **Lock 12 Historical Park.** Costumed docents explain the history of the site and the technology of the locks. Engineered by Henry Farnum under the direction of James Hillhouse and Eli Whitney, the canal was an astonishing feat for that period. For the schedule of the Lock Museum or for other park information, call the Cheshire Parks and Recreation Department at 272–2743.

EAST HAVEN

East of New Haven on the shore, this town is home to one of Connecticut's oldest and most popular family attractions. The efforts of the Branford Electric Railway Association have kept it alive and well, and as a result, the **Shoreline Trolley Museum** at 17 River Street still offers the same sense of old-time Connecticut that it did when I was a little girl riding its rails.

Nearly one hundred classic trolley cars are stored on the grounds and in the car barns of the property. Admission to the museum buys you unlimited 3-mile round-trip rides on the beautifully restored cars, plus a self-guided tour of the museum's display areas, which include the history of trolley technology and the local lines, plus some interactive and audiovisual exhibits. The trolley rides themselves are great fun, especially for young children, and special days are offered throughout the year, broadening the appeal for older kids. Among these are "haunted" rides in October; if you dare to take one of these ghoulish outings, be on the lookout for passengers who may have already passed to the Great Beyond.

You can picnic here and you can arrange birthday parties at a group discount. The regular season is Memorial Day to Labor Day from 11:00 A.M. to

5:00 P.M. In April they are open on Sundays only, and in May on Saturdays and Sundays. Weekend tours are offered throughout the fall as well. Admission is $5.00 for adults, $2.00 for children. Call 467–6927.

GUILFORD

One of Connecticut's oldest towns is Guilford, founded in the seventeenth century and famed for its exceptional town green. Today the green helps keep the center of Guilford looking much as it did in centuries past.

To reach the green, take Church Street south from the busy commercial strip on the Boston Post Road. At the end of Church Street, you will be at the head of the green. Several open acres crisscrossed by walkways make this a popular site to relax and to play.

When I was a child, my family came to Guilford in the summertime to see the **Guilford Handcrafts Exposition** on the Green. A three-day sale and celebration of the arts created by hundreds of juried craftspeople and displayed under tents, that tradition continues today in mid-July.

From Thursday to Saturday, the exposition features the work of about 350 artists, plus a small variety of entertainments such as storytellers, face painters, and usually a dance troupe or other live performances. A food concession sells unremarkable fare like hot dogs. We always pack a picnic.

Thousands of folks converge on the Green for this festival, which begins around midday and continues through the evening. This event is simply beautiful, and it's always a pleasure to admire the talents of the region's finest handcrafters.

The festival is organized by the local artists who form the backbone of the **Guilford Handcrafts Center,** north of Route 1 on Route 77. Comprised of a shop, a gallery, and a school, the Handcrafts Center is in itself a place to visit, but call first to see what's going on. For information on its options and the summer exposition, call 453–5947.

Right in the historic center of town are three homes representing life as experienced by the white settlers of the area in the seventeenth and eighteenth centuries. The most famous of these is the **Henry Whitfield State Museum,** the oldest stone house in New England and the oldest house in Connecticut. Built in 1639 by the Reverend Henry Whitfield, the post-medieval house has stone walls 3 feet thick and is the last remaining of four such houses strategically placed in Guilford as strongholds for the citizens during threat of war.

Now restored more as a museum than a period house, the structure contains an outstanding collection of furniture, housekeeping implements, textiles, weapons, and other artifacts of Connecticut history. The entire house is open to the public, as are the gardens and lawns. Among the collections displayed in the attic, you can see the 1726 Ebenezer Parmelee steeple clock, the first wooden works tower clock made in the colonies.

Located south of the Green at the corner of Old Whitfield Street and Stone House Lane, the museum is open for a mostly self-guided tour year-round Wednesday through Sunday, except Thanksgiving and December 15 to January 15. From April through October, the museum is open from 10:00 a.m to 5:00 p.m.; from November through March, it closes at 4:00 P.M. Admission is $3.00 for adults and $1.50 for children six to seventeen. For information, call 453–2457.

The other two historical homes are nearby on Boston Street, which leads east from the south side of the Green. The **Hyland House** at 84 Boston Street is our favorite of the three. Here visitors really do step into the eighteenth century, especially in the house's wonderful kitchen in the lean-to addition at the back of the house. How we wish the friendly docents would leave us alone to play here.

Though the house was built in 1660, the museum's focus is on the fifty to seventy-five years before the Revolutionary War. Everything that the family might have used during that period is here for your education. The architectural details and the collections in this house are among the finest in the state. Gorgeous paneling, wideboard floors, walk-in fireplaces, and artifacts of every sort are abundant throughout the house.

Cynthia Griswold, the curator for interpretation, is one of the best tour guides in the state (if you're lucky enough to get her). In tune with the interests of children of every age level, she makes the house come alive with scores of facts and stories. Naturally, the house's other docents follow her lead in this regard.

Open from 10:00 A.M. to 4:30 P.M. from early June to early September daily except Monday and on weekends from Labor Day to Columbus Day, the house is the site of a Historic Foodways Festival on the last full weekend in September. Hearthside cooking and other activities are among the special events designed for families. Admission is $2.00 for adults, and $1.50 for children twelve and older. For information, call 453–9477.

The third house is the 1774 **Thomas Griswold House** at 171 Boston Street. Greatly restored by the Guilford Keeping Society, it has a large number of important architectural details, including an original Guilford cupboard, a 10-foot-wide fireplace, and much more. This house also includes period rooms set with furnishings and implements in positions of use. Samplers, coverlets, costumes, dolls and toys, and a whimsical napkin ring collection are among the treasures here.

This house is also open daily except Monday from mid-June until early September and on weekends thereafter until Columbus Day. Tours, an antiques show, and an annual Civil War encampment are hosted on its grounds. On these special days the museum's blacksmith shop and barn are also open. Admission is $1.00 for all. For information, call 453–3176.

For those fatigued with art and history, a walk in the woods may be refreshing. Head to Guilford's **Westwoods Trails,** located less than a mile from the Green in an open-space area of more than 1,000 acres. Forty miles of trails lace through forest and marshland, some of which is still privately owned. Henry David Thoreau would have loved these trails. In 1862 he wrote, "I think that I cannot preserve my health and spirits, unless I spend four hours a day at least,—and it is commonly more than that,—sauntering through the woods and over the hills and fields, absolutely free from all worldly engagements."

Few of us are afforded the luxury of four-hour daily walks, but each of us should try this once a month on Connecticut's exceptional trails. Westwoods is a great place to start. Take Route 146 west from the Guilford Green to Sam Hill Road and park in the small lot right near that corner. Follow the white-blazed trail from that point and connect with any of the several other trails that lead to such points of interest as waterfalls, rock cliffs, colonial caves, an Indian cave, rock carvings, and vistas of the Sound and lake. The "G" Trail connects the Westwoods trails to the Stony Creek Quarry Preserve; here you can see the remains of old quarrying operations. The trails are open year-round at no charge from dawn to dusk. For information, call 453–8068.

HAMDEN

The most conspicuous feature of Hamden is in fact one of the most conspicuous features of all of Connecticut. Best viewed from a distance for the
fullest impact, the rounded hills of **Sleeping Giant State Park** look exactly like a figure in repose, its head toward the west, its chest and body
stretching eastward. (A great view is possible from I–91.)

Up close, the park is a great outdoor recreation area. Just off Route
10 several miles north of Hamden's business center, its 1,500 acres of
rolling woodland are traversed by hikers and cross-country skiers on 33
miles of trails. You can fish for trout in Mill River or you can hike the Tower
Trail, an easy walk on what is essentially a dirt road to the four-story stone
tower at the top of the ridge. You may also join one of the free guided trail
walks offered here mostly on Sundays in the spring and fall. Six to eight of
these are scheduled during these seasons at 1:30 P.M. The hike topics
include wildflowers, hawks, Giant lore, and more. For a hike schedule, call
the Sleeping Giant Park Association at 272–7841.

The park also offers a beautiful pine-canopied picnic grove with drinking water, restrooms, and grills. A small parking fee is charged in summer
on weekends and holidays. For information on these areas and the park in
general, call the Park Ranger Station at 789–7498.

Just north of the park, back out on Route 10, is **Wentworth Old-
Fashioned Ice Cream,** which is worth a drive from practically anywhere
if you like 100 percent natural, 16 percent butterfat ice cream. Owner
Chris Banos says the secret to Wentworth ice cream is no secret at all: "Just
buy quality." That philosophy plus a discerning sense of smell and taste
have led Chris to invent dozens of incredible flavors. Experimentation runs
amuck here, but not so far that it goes awry.

Ice cream, ices, yogurts, sherbets, twenty-four toppings and freshly
made cones, plus all kinds of fountain treats like egg creams and root beer
floats, are served up by friendly faces in this cheerfully painted parlor. If
you're willing to share, try Went-Berserk: eight sample scoops of ice cream
plus five toppings. Priced under $10, it's a great family deal, but Chris says
it's most popular with the college kids, who polish these off singlehandedly.

A make-your-own sundae bar was in the works the last time we
stopped by. After that, a birthday party room may be added inside; already

tables, a gazebo, and trellised arbors are outside in the summer. It is open daily from 11:00 A.M. to 10:30 P.M. in the summer; in the spring and fall, it closes around 9:00 P.M. From late November until roughly late February, it's closed. For information, call 281–7429.

Back down Route 10 toward the center of town is the **Eli Whitney Museum** at 915 Whitney Avenue. Not another historic home (even we have a limited capacity for these ubiquitous Connecticut treasures), this museum centers around the remaining and restored buildings of Whitneyville, a factory complex founded by Eli Whitney in the nineteenth century. On the site is a covered bridge, a wonderful outdoor Water Learning Lab, new exhibits inside the restored armory/gun factory, and an 1816 barn that offers a summer theater series and numerous folk concerts.

Open from noon to 5:00 P.M. Wednesday through Friday and Sunday, and from 10:00 A.M. to 3:00 P.M. Saturday, the exhibits in the armory focus on the scientific principles used by Whitney in his inventions, including interchangeable gun parts, the cotton gin, and more. A fascinating one-third scale model of the factory village once centered in this neighborhood is here as well. The museum hosts many special events and activities of interest to children. An extensive summer camp program offers excellent workhops and classes by registration only. Admission is charged. Call 777–1833.

MADISON

Perhaps the loveliest town on the New Haven County shoreline, Madison was one of Connecticut's earliest settlements. Once called East Guilford and connected geographically and politically to the town of Guilford, it was incorporated as a separate town in 1826. In previous centuries a fishing and shipbuilding center and later a seaside resort area, Madison is now primarily a residential suburb.

Many Madison families love this town because of its beautiful beaches. In fact, Connecticut's longest stretch of public beach is located here at **Hammonasset State Park,** off exit 62 of I–95. Enormously popular, the park offers a 2-mile beach, pavilions, picnic shelters, a 550-site campground, playing fields, a nature center with walking trails, a bike path, and sun, sand, rocks, and salty spray in abundance.

Day visitors and campers alike should stop at the **Meigs Point**

Nature Center. An excellent small facility, it has fresh- and saltwater aquariums, a marine touch tank, several well-executed dioramas, and a variety of live amphibians and reptiles of the area. Outside, the Willard's Island walking trail takes you out through the salt meadow and onto Willard's Island, once farmed in colonial times and now home to red cedar and sassafras trees and the small mammals and birds of the marshlands. Fourteen stations explain the flora and fauna, including the nesting sites of the beautiful ospreys that soar overhead in spring, summer, and fall.

The Nature Center rangers provide walks, talks, slide presentations, and craft workshops for children on a regular schedule all summer long. The Junior Naturalist program for children nine to twelve and the Outdoor Explorer program for six- to eight-year-olds include activities like fishing, crabbing, seining, birding, and bat house building.

Held midweek in July and August, the program is open to drop-in visitors; those who complete four sessions receive a certificate for their achievement. Wear bug repellent, sunscreen, and old shoes. The center programs are free to all, but they are also funded entirely by donation, so feel free to support the exceptional work of this tireless team.

The campground is a great seaside vacation spot—well-run, very clean, and beautiful in all seasons. The sites are almost all open, so if you like the hills and woods, you are in the wrong park. Bring a metal tub or fire ring (or rent one here); there are no grills or firepits, and campfires are only permitted in metal containers. Campfire programs, bingo, an occasional dance, and a children's playground with swings and a great wooden ship are part of what you'll enjoy here. Bring bikes and rollerblades—the campground has excellent lanes for both sports.

The park is open year-round. Activities are held in summer only. A per-vehicle admission charge is required from Memorial Day to Labor Day, plus a few weekends past Labor Day. For information, call 245–2785.

Madison itself has a nice variety of shops and restaurants, plus two restored or partially restored historic homes. The Allis–Bushnell House and the Deacon John Grave House are both open to the public at varying times throughout the year. Some of the shops are especially appealing to kids; among these are The Bay Window, The General Store, and R. J. Julia's

Booksellers. Don't skip town without stopping at **Marie's Sweet Shop** on the Boston Post Road. This little pink storefront with the park bench out front has terrific homemade ice cream, great chocolates, and all the fountain treats you'd expect from an independent ice-cream emporium. The best ice cream on the shoreline is made right here.

MIDDLEBURY

Way out in the hills that rise toward Litchfield County and the Berkshires is the pretty community of Middlebury, home of the state's one and only remaining amusement park. Located on Route 64 on the shores of Lake Quassapaug, **Quassy Amusement Park** is a sort of old-fashioned affair similar to the Savin Rock Amusement Park old-timers may remember in West Haven. Not as sleek and sophisticated as other New England amusement centers like Rhode Island's Rocky Point or Massachusetts' Riverside, Quassy is still a whole lot of fun for families, especially those with young children.

More than twenty-five rides, a miniature golf course, a narrow-gauge miniature railway, and a swimming and picnic area on the shores of the lake are here to enjoy weekends in April through May and daily through Labor Day. You can ride the carousel (a beautiful fiberglass reproduction of the original), two roller coasters, bumper cars, and all kinds of carnival-style rides like the Whip, the Monster, and the Himalayas. Along with these are arcades, games of chance and skill, and a special area for children under age five. We picnicked on the day we came, but you can purchase lots of foods in the park, from the great American hot dog to barbecued chicken. As long as you're not expecting Disney World, you're bound to have a good time here.

Carload days, bargain days, and group rates make Quassy affordable for most families. Regular rates are $9.95 per person for an all-rides/all-day pass, plus a $3.00 parking fee per car. Carload days are $20.00 per carload, plus parking. On Friday nights all rides, are just 25 cents apiece. After 5:00 P.M. any night, a rides pass is $5.50 per person; on Mondays and Wednesdays in July and August, an all-day pass is $6.95. For information, call (800) FOR–PARK or 758–2913.

NEW HAVEN

Once the site of a Native American village called *Quinnipiac,* which means "long river place," New Haven was renamed by English settlers who established a colony here in 1640. Since its earliest days an important center of industry, education, and culture, New Haven remains one of the most vital cities in the state. An excellent place for families to visit, this city has many wonderful destinations, but I was able to choose only a handful of those you might consider. Be certain to call the Greater New Haven Convention and Visitors Bureau (800–332–7829) to ask for a copy of their terrific guide to the city and its 'burbs.

You might want to start a day in New Haven high above the city in its **West Rock Ridge State Park.** Overlooking the entire city (and the Sound and many other parts of Connecticut on a clear day), West Rock is one of two ridges of basalt forced skyward through volcanic action some 200 million years ago. **East Rock,** its twin on the other side of the city, is recognizable by its matching sandstone cliffs; that park is city-owned and has trails, a bird sanctuary, and a playground you might enjoy.

West Rock Ridge State Park runs along the top of the western ridge and has a variety of recreational areas, including hiking trails, a fishing pond called Lake Wintergreen, and a picnic area. Its blue-blazed main trail, called **Regicides Trail,** is accessible at the top of the ridge via a scenic drive or you can walk in from the Nature Center (see below). This trail offers beautiful views of the harbor and leads through very scenic woodlands. One of the most infamous sites here is the **Judges Cave,** where in 1661 Edward Whalley and William Goffe hid from bounty hunters hoping to claim the £100 reward for their capture as traitors against the Crown, the two having signed a death warrant against Charles I years earlier.

The **West Rock Nature Center** is a separate area just north of the entrance to the park on Wintergreen Avenue. Owned and operated by the city, its forty acres include shorter nature trails that take you past the ravine, a small waterfall, and so on; you can also visit the Nature House with wildlife displays such as native birds, reptiles, and small mammals. The center also has a picnic shelter and restrooms. If you come in wintertime with your toboggans, a guaranteed good time awaits you here.

West Rock Ridge State Park is open year-round daily from 8:00 A.M.

to sunset. The southern portion of the scenic drive is open to motor vehicles only on a seasonal basis; call for opening dates. The northern section is closed to vehicles but open to hikers, cyclists, and skiers year-round. Folks in cars wishing to hike in winter can park at the Nature Center. West Rock Nature Center is open Monday through Friday from 10:00 A.M. to 4:00 P.M., except holidays. Admission is free. The Nature Center entrance is on Wintergreen Avenue, not far from exit 59 off Route 15. The park entrance is about 200 feet south of the Nature Center entrance, also on Wintergreen Avenue. For information, call 787–8016 or 789–7498.

Drop down into the center of the city after this bird's-eye view and check out the many riches of Yale University. These next paragraphs represent a whirlwind tour and in fact give just a taste of the many opportunities for family adventure and edification you can gain here.

Located on opposite sides of Chapel Street between York and High streets are the **Yale University Art Gallery** and the **Yale Center for British Art.** The former is the oldest university art museum in the United States; the latter is the largest collection of British art outside of the United Kingdom. Both are marvelous, both are free, and both have much to offer to families, who should visit often.

The Center for British Art is very serious and "stuffier" than the other; many of its free lectures and symposia are best suited to adults and students, but children are more than welcome to the museum proper and to all gallery tours, concerts, and films. Programs especially for children occasionally appear on the center's calendar of events. Its gift shop is wonderful and very child-oriented.

The Art Gallery is also very fine and serious, but its collection extends from ancient to modern art and somehow, as a result, seems more palatable to children, at least in that the scene changes more markedly from gallery to gallery. This museum also hosts a variety of tours, programs, and concerts, many designed to appeal to families.

Both museums are open year-round Tuesday through Saturday from 10:00 A.M. to 5:00 P.M. and Sunday from noon to 5:00 P.M. For information on both, call 432–2800.

The Yale Collection of Musical Instruments at 15 Hillhouse Avenue (between Trumbull and Grove) is open September through June only Tuesday through Thursday from 1:00 to 4:00 p.m., a schedule that makes it mighty hard to take the kids here. But if you have a child who really loves music, this awe-inspiring collection is well worth a day out of school. More than 800 European and American instruments from the sixteenth to twentieth centuries are on display, and an annual concert series is offered to boot. The museum suggests a donation of $1.00; concert tickets cost extra. For information, call 432–0822.

If you are here in the summertime on Friday night at 7:00 p.m., grab a blanket and a picnic dinner and head to **Harkness Tower** near the Old Campus between Chapel and Elm. There in the courtyard, relax for a while and listen to the incredible music of the carillon. Students of the art as well as international artists play here several times each summer for about an hour. I love this series. Don't pack anything crunchy in your picnic and make sure you close your eyes for the full and unforgettable effect of the glorious classical pieces on each concert's program. This also is free. For a schedule of performances, call 432–4158.

Last in the Yale neighborhood is one of the most popular family destinations in the state—the **Peabody Museum of Natural History** at 170 Whitney Avenue. Everybody has probably already been here, so I won't linger at this point. For those who have not, just think dinosaurs, dinosaurs, dinosaurs, plus animals, Indians, seashells, rocks, minerals, mummies, mastodons, and much, much more. Special events, classes, workshops, and hands-on activities are offered throughout the year.

Open year-round daily except Monday (with the exception of some holiday Mondays when it is open at regular hours), the museum hours are 10:00 A.M. to 5:00 P.M. and Sunday noon to 5:00 P.M. Admission is $4.00 for adults and $2.50 for children three to fifteen. Admission is free to everyone Tuesday through Friday from 3:00 to 5:00 P.M. For information, call 432–5050.

Families with young children should visit the **Connecticut Children's Museum** at 22 Wall Street. A play-space more than a museum, this bright and spacious facility is perfect for children under the age of eight, plus any older siblings not too embarrassed to join in the fun. Each area of the museum represents a part of a neighborhood: a hospital, a restaurant, a post office, a gas station, and a grocery store are available for kids to pretend in for as long as they want—just be sure to take turns.

You can construct a building with giant blocks, make a call on an old switchboard, or create a craft in the arts center. Something fun is always on the schedule, including storytellings, sing-alongs, puppet shows, and parades. Children participate in all of these.

Open year-round except for about three weeks in September, the museum hours are 10:00 A.M. to 2:00 P.M. Tuesday through Thursday and 10:00 A.M. to 4:00 P.M. Saturday and Sunday. Admission is $3.00 for everyone. For information, call 562–5437.

New Haven is not often characterized as a city on the sea, but it is a port, and some of the best the city has to offer is by the shore or on the Sound. Sadly polluted, New Haven's harbor is not known for its beaches, but the city does have a great seaside park and swimming area out beyond the worst pollution. Popular with city residents and birdwatchers, **Lighthouse Point Park** is open to the public year-round from 6:00 A.M. to sunset, free of charge except from Memorial Day to Labor Day when each carload pays $2.00. You reach it from the Woodward Avenue exit off I–95; follow the signs down Townsend Avenue to the park.

Once the enormously popular last stop on the New Haven Trolley line, the park had bathhouses, boat rides, and baseball games, with such legends as Babe Ruth and Ty Cobb playing here Sunday afternoons during the Roaring Twenties. Nearly destroyed in the hurricane of 1938, the park later was home to a small amusement park. Now only one of its famed rides remains, and it is a beauty. Housed in a New Haven landmark building on the National Register of Historic Places is the **Lighthouse Point Carousel,** an astonishingly well-restored treasure and a joy to ride.

Assembled around 1911 from new and used parts of other carousels, it operates from Memorial Day to Labor Day Tuesday through Friday from 3:00 to 7:00 P.M. and on Saturday and Sunday from 11:00 A.M. to 7:00 P.M. It is closed on Monday except for holidays. For 50 cents per ride, you can hop on any one of these seventy Coney Island–style steeds, with names like Wild Wind, Sweet Sue, City Lights, Sea Dreamer, and Sundance. The antique murals at the top of the carousel depict scenes from the history of New Haven; the Stinson Organ plays heavenly music. Group reservations are accepted—what a great place to party.

The park has a pre–Civil War lighthouse and a great little nature center at the East Shore Ranger Station. It has a marine touch-tank and a ship's deck to pretend on. You may learn something about marine ecology and maritime history at a program here. Say hi to Ranger Phil Vallie for me.

The park's beach is clean and safe; a snack bar, spotless changing rooms and showers, a small wooden playground, and several swing-sets are here. A boat launch, volleyball nets, a nature trail, and several excellent bird-watching areas are also in the park. Hawk watching during the annual migration from late August through November brings birders from all over the state. For information, you can call the Park Manager at 787–8005 or the Ranger Station at 787–8790.

After you leave Lighthouse Point, you might want to make a quick stop at Black Rock Fort and Fort Nathan Hale. As you travel north again on Townsend Avenue, take a left on Fort Hale Park Road. **Black Rock Fort** was built in 1776 by order of the Connecticut Colony to protect the Port of New Haven from the British. Unfortunately, by the time the British arrived in 1779, only nineteen defenders remained at the fort; they were swiftly captured by the enemy, who then marched on to New Haven.

Fort Nathan Hale was built near the same site in the early 1800s, as the British and Americans prepared again to fight. This time, during the War of 1812, the defenders successfully repelled the British invaders. Rebuilt in 1863 with new ramparts, bunkers, a drawbridge, and eighteen guns, the fort was prepared for Civil War action, but it never came. Now you can take a self-guided tour of both sites. The drawbridge, its moat, the ramparts, bunkers, and other fortifications either still exist or have been restored. It's a neat site, but it's very low-key. The folks who maintain the fort hope someday to have a visitor's center with multidimensional educational displays, but for now that's all just on the drawing board. Come any day from Memorial Day to Labor Day from 10:00 A.M. to 4:00 P.M. Admission is free. For information, call 787–8790.

If you want to see New Haven from the Sound and get a history and ecology lesson and a great boat ride to boot, call **Schooner, Inc.** from April through November at 865–1737. They'll take you out on chartered half-day, full-day, and sunset sails aboard the *Quinnipiack,* a 91-foot gaff-rigged wooden schooner. If that's too expensive, try the ***Liberty Belle*** at

562–4163. This motor vessel offers day and evening cruises of the harbor and shoreline with narrated tours on some rides.

If you need food, try **Pepe's** or **Sally's** pizzerias on Wooster Street. No better pizza has ever been made. For great vegetarian lunches close to the Art Gallery, I like **Claire's Corner Copia Cafe** at College and Chapel streets. The kids might also think 1950s-style **Spanky's** is fun; it's on the corner of Crown and College. Wherever you eat, you might want to skip dessert and stop instead at **Sugar Magnolia,** an incredible candy shop on Chapel just west of College. Ohmigod.

WATERBURY

Known for nearly two centuries as one of the nation's most important industrial cities, Waterbury is also one of Connecticut's best embodiments of the term "melting pot." For 300 years its citizenry has been among the most diverse of all Connecticut populations, as wave after wave of immigrants has come here in search of the American Dream.

Though their toil in the factories and mills of Waterbury was often far from idyllic, many of these workers would say their dream did come true. This success is evident in the thriving neighborhoods, the beautiful turn-of-the-century architecture, and a rich variety of cultural entities.

Excellent for families wishing to expand their appreciation for the unique contributions the little state of Connecticut has made to American culture, the newly renovated **Mattatuck Museum** shows off its valuable collection at 144 West Main Street on the Waterbury Green. This dramatic and engaging museum is elaborately designed to enhance the "museum experience" for children even though it contains only the works of Connecticut artists and exhibits only about the history of the Brass Capitol of the World.

The Mattatuck, in fact, is the only museum in Connecticut that has selected the works in its art galleries entirely from the accomplishments of American masters who have been associated with Connecticut. This exclusivity is not at all a drawback. It allows visitors to celebrate both Connecticut artists and Connecticut themes through the works of John Trumbull, William Jennys, Frederic Church, Maurice Prendergast, Alexander Calder, and many others.

In the Brass Roots history exhibit, you can examine a re-created seventeenth-century house frame, wander through a nineteenth-century boardinghouse re-creation that has the voices of immigrants telling their stories, and explore a nineteenth-century brass mill while listening to the voices of workers describing their workdays in the factory. Like a time-travel machine, this exhibit transports you backward through two centuries.

In this same area you will learn of the amazing number of products that originated in the industries of Waterbury and other towns of western Connecticut. This exhibit proudly displays the clocks, watches, buttons, cameras, tableware, rubber products, and furniture that made the Naugatuck Valley one of the most productive areas of the nation during and after the Industrial Revolution.

The Mattatuck also contains a museum store, a cafe, and a courtyard garden. Open year-round Tuesday through Saturday from 10:00 A.M. to 5:00 P.M. It is also open Sunday from noon to 5:00 except in July and August. Admission is free. For information, call 753–0381.

MIDDLESEX COUNTY

If you were to stand on the bare, windblown summit of Great Hill in the Meshomasic State Forest, you would be easily convinced that Middlesex is the most beautiful county in Connecticut. On a clear day, the waters of Long Island Sound glimmer far to the south. Four hundred feet below you, Great Hill Pond laps at the forest. And out of the north curls the broad ribbon of the Connecticut River on its way to the sea. The small country charms of the northeastern counties are eclipsed by this spectacular vista that reveals the best features of the region. From sea to river to vernal ponds, Middlesex County is a land shaped by water.

Also shaped by the sea and the river have been the lives of the inhabitants of these shores. Many of the attractions in these parts are closely linked to the cultures and industries that developed in response to the geography. Come to Middlesex for saltwater taffy, seafood of every sort, steamboat rides, covered bridges, raft races, and riverside rendezvous. Enjoy the bounty of the county's forests and farms—the water has nourished these well, and the riches they yield are jewels in Connecticut's crown.

CHESTER

Though we've decided upon an alphabetical arrangement of towns for the format of this book, it's a bit awkward to start a tour of Middlesex County

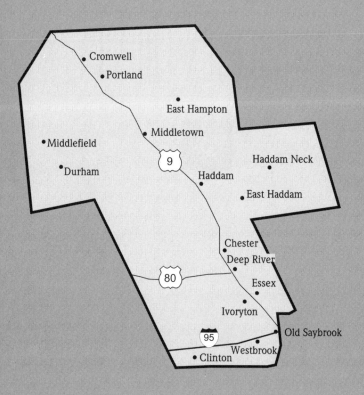

Cromwell
Portland
East Hampton
Middletown
Middlefield
9
Durham
Haddam Neck
Haddam
East Haddam
Chester
Deep River
80
Essex
Ivoryton
95
Old Saybrook
Westbrook
Clinton

Middlesex County

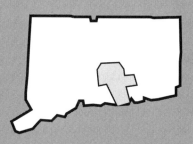

with Chester. It is not exactly the family entertainment center of the county. Quiet, quaint, and *tiny,* it falls first on the list of towns, however, and is
host to one of the most captivating summer performance series your family might ever see. So here we begin.

Located on Route 148 and surrounded by Cockaponset State Forest,
Chester was founded in 1692 as Pattaquonk Quarter, the fourth parish of
Saybrook. An independent town by 1836, it seems content to remain in
the nineteenth century. Its winding lanes lined with historic buildings are
unblemished by purveyors of fast food, slushy red soft drinks, or other
atrocities of modern civilization. In Chester you will find lovely shops,
great restaurants, and serenity.

On four Sundays in June, you will also find **The National Theater of
the Deaf** performing on the village green. In my opinion, these hour-long
free performances are worth a day's journey. Mesmerizing, life-affirming,
mystical, magical, and superbly executed, the stories that flow from the fin-
gertips of the actors will amuse and amaze the entire family.

Founded in the mid-1960s, this provocative and inspiring company
of deaf and hearing actors has set a standard of excellence that guarantees
it a full house in performances in every state and throughout the world.
Don't miss the opportunity to experience at least one of its powerful and
beautiful storytellings. Performances are usually held outdoors at 2:00 P.M.
at the Chester Meetinghouse on the green. Follow signs to the
Meetinghouse from the village center. For information, call 526–4971
(voice) or 526–4974 (TTY).

If you arrive in the area on Saturday, pick up a Sunday picnic lunch
at **The Wheatmarket** at 4 Water Street, 'round the back of the main village lane. The proprietors close on Sundays to spend time with their own
families, but Monday through Saturday from 9:00 A.M. to 6:00 P.M. they
serve delicious sandwiches, soups, cheeses, and breads.

If you can't resist a peek at the shops, I recommend one in particular:
Connecticut River Artisans at 1 Spring Street. This cooperative showcases the traditional and contemporary work of local craftspeople.
Furniture, pottery, jewelry, sculpture, and more in all media are here. The
prices are upscale, but luckily, it costs nothing to enjoy the artistry.

CROMWELL

Cromwell has a mini-attraction kids absolutely love. **Amy's Udder Joy Farm** at 27 North Road is one of those places I thought I could write about without seeing. It's a backyard/barnyard petting zoo, after all. Straightforward stuff, sort of like a day off for a travel writer. Kick off the Keds and write it straight from the armchair.

No such luck. When I told my kids that owner Amy O'Toole had a llama, a yak, pot-belly pigs, black-belly sheep, African pygmy hedgehogs, and Tennessee fainting goats, they were in the car, ready to go, before I could say "and, now, for something completely different . . .."

Adjacent to her husband's farm where Holstein cows and Yorkshire pigs reside, Amy keeps forty or more rare, primitive, exotic, or endangered species from around the world. It seems that only Doctor Dolittle himself and the pushmi-pullyu are missing. The only zoo of any sort in these parts, Amy's farm is also educational. Signs on all the pens or tanks let you know what you're looking at, and someone is always around to add to your education. All drop-in visitors are welcome, but groups should call ahead if a lectured tour is desired. Amy likes to plan ahead to avoid crowding in this quarter-acre menagerie.

The indoor and outdoor exhibits include more than one hundred animals, plus approximately 200 chickens, geese, peacocks, and ducks, all of which are also rare or exotic. You can buy feed at coin-operated machines, and you can actually pet or hold many of the animals. The indoor barn exhibits include various mammals, reptiles, arachnids, and small rock, mineral, fossil, and butterfly collections.

The farm offers an added attraction. Every weekend children can ride the state's one and only living carousel. Four ponies are decked out with special hair-duds, pretty blankets, and jeweled saddles and bridles. Amy plays calliope music over the loudspeakers, and the ponies give delighted young children four turns around the riding ring. I hoped to avoid the word "cute" in this book, but this is very, very cute.

Amy's Udder Joy is open from early to mid-April (depending on the snow and mud) through Labor Day, Wednesday through Sunday 11:00 A.M. to 5:00 P.M. After Labor Day until the last weekend in October, the farm is open only on weekends at those same hours. Admission for each

The presence of a llama, a yak, miniature pot-belly pigs, and African pygmy hedgehogs prove that Amy's Udder Joy Farm is not your average petting zoo. (Photo by Amy O'Toole/Courtesy Amy's Udder Joy Farm)

person over the age of one is $2.00, and pony rides are an additional $2.00. And yes—the goats really do faint. Amazing. For information and directions to 27 North Road in Cromwell, call 635–3924.

DEEP RIVER

I love the name of this town. Deep River. When I first heard the name as a child on a family daytrip to Gillette's Castle, I thought Tom Sawyer must live in this town. Somewhere, he sits dangling his feet in the water, chewing on a piece of straw and watching the steamboats pass by.

Nearly thirty years later, Deep River is not much different than it was the first time I saw it. And it still has a great family-style event every third Saturday in July—the **Deep River Muster of Ancient Fife and Drum Corps.** A gathering of up to seventy separate corps from all over the nation and a few from overseas, it includes a long and colorful parade up the town's Main Street (Route 154). Arrive early. Chairs and blankets line the parade route long before the first salute is sounded. Authentic uniforms, unforgettable music, and even bagpipers, pirates, Uncle Sam, and Dan'l Boone are part of the show.

After the parade, which can easily last two hours, walk to Devitt Field at the bottom of the parade route. The corps meet there for food and drink and special performances. You can buy fifes, drums, tri-cornered hats, and other related items in the tents lining the perimeter of the field. You can even find out how to join a corps. The parade and admission to the field are free, but parking will cost you $5.00 in one of the "lots" set up on the lawns of the townsfolk. For information, call 767–2237.

Deep River has a terrific one-stop shopping secret, also on Route 154 at what the postal service calls 39 Main Street. Open seven days a week from 10:00 A.M. to 5:00 p.m., the **Great American Trading Company** is a factory store that sells wooden toys and games, marbles by the pound, wooden boxes, puzzles, puppets, rubber stamps, and much more.

You can pick up great gifts here—checker sets, mancala boards, pick-up sticks, yo-yos—all at wonderful prices. Buy first-quality, seconds, or put your own set together. You can pick out your own colored glass stones and a mancala board for about $6.00; my favorite children's catalog sells a similar product for $14.95. I stock up here twice yearly. Santa himself ought to shop here. Plus, the elves who work in the store are really nice. For information, call 526–4335.

DURHAM

Durham has some of the prettiest farmland in the county. Centered on Route 17 just south of Middletown, it is famed for these farms, for its beautiful historical residences—and for its Fair.

The **Durham Fair** is held the third weekend in September right in the center of town. The fairgrounds are hardly noticeable most of the year as you drive past the green, but for three days annually, the joint is hoppin'. Like all country fairs, Durham Fair celebrates the culture and traditions of local agriculture through literally hundreds of exhibits, demonstrations, and food and craft booths.

The largest country fair currently held in Connecticut, it displays sheep, cattle, draft animals, and every other barn and farm animal you can name. Look at quilts, pies, fruits, and flowers. Ride the Ferris wheel and go through the fun house. Eat candied apples, hot cashews, and strawberry-topped Belgian waffles. Wander through the antique farm machinery museum and buy something at the antiques show.

Over the aroma of fried everything rise the sounds of country music, announcements of contest winners, and screams from the midway. If your family has sleek, sophisticated city ways, put them aside for a day and come to the fair for a down-home good time. The ballet can wait, and your kids should really see the oxen and draft horses. They are a tribute to bio-diversity, evolution, or Supreme Intelligence. Whatever your belief system, you have to be amazed by these creatures.

The fair runs for three days, beginning at 9:00 A.M. on the Friday of the third week in September. Admission is $5.00 per adult; children under twelve are free. A free shuttle bus to and from free parking in various lots is also available. Call 349–9495.

EAST HADDAM

This river town has one of Connecticut's most famous attractions—**Gillette's Castle,** at 67 River Road. I have yet to find a Connecticut guide-book that can resist mentioning this medieval-looking wonder. Toured by 100,000 visitors each year, the castle is so popular with families that many of you have probably already been here.

For those of you who have not, this splendid fieldstone fortress sits on a bluff called the Seventh Sister, high above the eastern bank of the Connecticut River. Completed in 1919 as the home of actor William Gillette (famed for his stage portrayal of Sherlock Holmes in the early part of the twentieth century), the house was built according to the exact spec-ifications of its somewhat eccentric owner. The turrets, terraces, archways, and fountains found outside are awesome enough, but the interior will make you gape. The twenty-four rooms, each more unusual than the last, contain gorgeous stonework, extraordinary hand-carved woodwork, and many of Gillette's original furnishings and possessions.

The castle also contains a re-creation of Sherlock Holmes's sitting room at 221B Baker Street, London, and an incredible assemblage of Holmes-related memorabilia, the largest such collection in the world. I must say that, as a child, both the woodwork and the Holmesiana escaped me entirely. I was imagining Arthur and Guinevere and Morgan Le Fay, Robin Hood and Maid Marian and Will Scarlet, wishing all the tourists would go away and let me pretend.

The castle grounds are part of the 200-acre **Gillette's Castle State Park,** an area of breathtaking views of the river and valley. Three and a half miles of trails allow you to explore, and you'll find many spots perfect for picnicking, napping, or playing knights and ladies. Primitive campsites (with flush toilets and drinking water) are available near the river for canoeists.

The park is open year-round from 8:00 A.M. to sunset; no fee is charged for enjoying the grounds. The castle is open from 10:00 A.M. to 5:00 P.M. every day from the Saturday of Memorial Day weekend through Columbus Day, and weekends only, from 10:00 A.M. to 4:00 P.M., from the weekend after Columbus Day through the weekend before Christmas. During the four weekends between Thanksgiving and the week before Christmas, the castle has a Victorian Holiday Celebration. Special decorations, musical performances, and other entertainments are offered. Tours of the castle cost $4.00 for adults and $2.00 for children six through eleven; children five and under are free. For information, call 526–2336.

If you arrived at the castle via the western side of Route 82, you crossed the river on the longest swinging bridge in New England (it pivots to a position parallel to the banks so boats can pass). You also passed the **Goodspeed Opera House** at Goodspeed Landing. I know you noticed this building. It's huge, it's white, and it looks like someone in 1876 was trying to create the biggest, best Second Empire opera house in the nation.

Restored inside and out, the Goodspeed presents hit musical productions from April through December. Mostly revivals of Broadway favorites from the 1920s through the 1960s, the shows are great family entertainment. We recently saw a fabulous production of *Shenandoah;* the scenery alone was outstanding, and everything else was grand.

Tours of the Opera House are offered Saturdays and Mondays in season; call for specific times and reservations. For $2.00 per adult and $1.00 for children under twelve, you get to see the dressing rooms and all the inner workings, plus you hear great stories of the Goodspeed's illustrious past. For show information, call 873–8668; for tour information, call 873–8664.

Another great stop in East Haddam is **Devil's Hopyard State Park** on Route 156. Beautiful in all seasons, its moderate trails through heavily wooded terrain are wonderful for families. Views of the countryside are especially lovely in the fall, but the 60-foot cascades of Chapman Falls are most impressive in the spring. Look for the potholes in the rocks at the base of the falls. Legend says that these formations were made by the hot hoofs of the Devil as he hopped from ledge to ledge so as not to get wet.

Twenty-one wooded campsites with drinking water and outhouses are available here. You can also fish from the streams and picnic wherever you like. The park is open year-round from 8:00 A.M. to sunset. Leave well before dark if you believe the stories that this wood is haunted by the Devil and the ancient hags of Haddam. For the full scoop, call 873-8566.

EAST HAMPTON

Near the shores of Lake Pocotopaug is the tiny hamlet of East Hampton, the town in which I took my first childhood family vacation, saw my first snapping turtle, and learned both how to canoe and how to capsize a canoe. Whoops!

I also remember that somewhere near there, I visited a perfume factory—took a tour, in fact, and brought home samples in tiny vials. I can't find a trace of what that place might have been, so if any of you remember what I remember, drop me a line at Globe Pequot. I'm dying to know if memory has served me correctly. Even my mother stares at me when I recollect this, as though perhaps it's more likely that I was part of some extraterrestrial laboratory experience the rest of the family escaped.

South of the town itself, on Route 151, is **Hurd State Park,** another of the excellent facilities the state maintains for public use. Like other state parks, it is typically beautiful, clean, safe, and fun. It's special because of its location overlooking the Connecticut River and its pretty Hurd Brook Gorge. Its recreational opportunities, include rock climbing, snowmobiling, cross-country skiing, freshwater fishing, and hiking.

Campsites are available for youth groups and for boaters. Many campers canoe from here to Gillette's Castle State Park or **Selden Neck State Park,** a 528-acre island downriver toward Lyme; accessible only by boat, those parks also have primitive riverside campsites available May through September. The state has provided toilets and drinking water at Gillette's Castle and Hurd; drinking water, outhouses, and fireplaces are at Selden Neck. No admission fee is charged at any time for day use of Hurd or Selden Neck, but overnight camping fees are charged at all three facilities. For information, call 526–2336.

You might recall that in the introduction to this county I mentioned **Great Hill** in the Meshomasic State Forest. It is from the Cobalt section of East Hampton that you will reach it. Drive to the intersection of Routes 151 and 66 in Cobalt, and go east on Route 66 just a bit over a mile to Cones Hill Road. Take a left on Cones Hill Road and drive 1 mile to its junction with Clark Hill and Great Hill roads. Take the right fork onto Clark Hill Road and drive a little more than a half-mile until you see a dirt service road (which may be marked Forest Road) on the left. A tad more than half a mile up the dirt service road, you will come to the Shenipsit Trail, which is marked by blue blazes. Park at that crossing and hike south (toward the left, from where you met the crossing) about 1 3/4 miles on the trail. At that point, the Shenipsit main trail turns left, and a white-blazed trail toward the south will take you several hundred feet to the summit of Great Hill. You'll retrace your steps to your car. This is a moderate hike of about 4 miles round trip. For information, call the Connecticut Forest and Park Association at 346–2372.

ESSEX

I love Essex, especially at the height of summer and in the stillness of winter. Elegant, and gracious, Essex is another of Connecticut's windows on the past. Three-masted schooners, whale-oil lamps, scrimshaw, taverns with steaming bowls of chowder—these are the stuff of Essex's past.

Today, Essex offers a reminder of all of that. Its concentration of eighteenth- and nineteenth-century homes on narrow village lanes, its wharf and marinas, its shops and restaurants—all are evocative of earlier centuries when Essex was one of the busiest ports on the Connecticut River. Stop with the kids at the **Griswold Inn** on Main Street for a meat pie in winter at a table near one of the fireplaces. Stroll through the streets decorated with thousands of little white lights. Hope for snow. You'll come back year after year.

Make sure you stop at the **Connecticut River Museum** at the foot of Main Street at Steamboat Dock. It is a small but top-notch facility, presenting the history of the Connecticut River from its geology to its inhabitants, its industries, and the cultures that developed in the area because of the river. Scale models of some of the river's most famous warships, steamboats, and pleasure crafts are displayed along with shipbuilding tools, marine art, and fascinating archaeological artifacts unearthed in the area. A working replica of the first submarine, the *American Turtle,* is here.

Every year between Thanksgiving and New Year's Day, the curators prepare an exhibition of special interest to children. The exhibits of the past three years have been dollhouses and miniatures, snow globes, and model trains. In summer, workshops, concerts, and camp-type activities are planned for children. For a week or two in the summer of 1995, a 94-foot schooner will be dockside for public sails and hands-on learning activities. The curators look forward to making that visit an annual event. Call the number below for specific information.

The museum is open year-round Tuesday through Sunday from 10:00 A.M. to 5:00 P.M. and is closed Mondays and major holidays. Adult admission is $4.00; children nine through twelve pay $2.00, and children under nine are free. For information, call 767–8269.

Essex is also home to one of Connecticut's most popular family tourist activities—the **Essex Steam Train and Riverboat Ride,** offered by the Valley Railroad Company. On a typical daily run, these beautifully restored vintage steam locomotives and rail cars take passengers on a 12-mile round-trip ride from Essex to Deep River. At Deep River Landing, you can opt to board the triple-decker riverboat for a cruise upriver past Gillette's Castle to the East Haddam Bridge and the Goodspeed Opera House and then back downriver. The trip takes about two and a half hours if you also take the boat ride.

These rides are both fun and educational. Each segment of the train/boat ride includes an entertaining narration about the railroad and the steamship lines. The sights and sounds are wonderful. Bells, whistles, tooting of important proportions, and the clickety-clack of the railroad track are accompanied by the shouts of blue-capped conductors calling, "All aboard!"

Special events include a Ghost Train in October and the North Pole

Express in December. These are popular family and birthday party–type excursions. Santa, Mrs. Claus, and lots of elves are aboard the Express, with surprises for every child. Who knows what passengers ride the Gho—oo—oost Train, but I assure you they have surprises, too.

The trainyard is on Route 154, about a quarter-mile from Route 9, exit 3. Visit the station, the car-barns, and the gift shop before or after your ride. Enjoy the old-fashioned fun from mid-May through October, plus the North Pole Express. Special events and combinations are offered regularly and fares vary, so call for information at 767–0103.

HADDAM

The Connecticut River beckons to visitors once again in Haddam, this time on the west bank (right off Route 82 at the bridge), where **Camelot Cruises** docks their 400–passenger triple-decker cruise ship. Families can take two-hour "Ramblin' River" cruises that include a lively narration about the sights along the river, plus live jazz entertainment. Beverages and light lunches can also be purchased on board or at the Dockside Restaurant. The cruises cost approximately $13.00 per adult, $5.50 per child ages five to eleven, and are free to under-fives. Cruises depart daily at 1:30 P.M. from June 15 through October 31.

Camelot also offers all-day cruises to Sag Harbor, Long Island, from late June through Labor Day. Bring a bicycle along or walk to the many shops, restaurants, museums, and historic sites of Sag Harbor. A typical trip leaves Haddam at 9:00 A.M. and returns at 6:00 P.M. Adults pay approximately $23.00; children under twelve are half that, and under-fives are free. These trips sail on Tuesday, Wednesday, Thursday, and Sunday.

Murder mystery, fall foliage, and dinner and brunch cruises are also available. Reservations are necessary for those cruises and for groups at any time. Schedules and fares change, so call for information at 345–8591.

Haddam is also the site of one of the best Native American festivals in the country. Held annually at Haddam Meadows State Park on Route 154, the **Quinnehtukqut Rendezvous and Native American Festival** is an extraordinary event that brings together Native Americans from all over the nation for three days of dancing and drum competitions, arts and crafts demonstrations, museum displays, storytelling, black powder and archery contests, and booths of Native American foods and crafts for sale.

In addition, living-history demonstrators set up camp to portray the Fur Trade period prior to 1840; in these authentic encampments, visitors can observe the habits, fashions, crafts, and trades of pre–Civil War settlers.

This festival provides an excellent glimpse into the heritage and traditions of Native Americans of the seventeenth and eighteenth centuries. Their authentic tipis, furnishings, and costumes positioned side by side with the encampments of the "mountain men" have a tremendous impact. Strolling through sections representing the Revolutionary War period, the French and Indian War period, and the Fur Trade period, you will see candlemaking, tinsmithing, spinning, flint knapping, sacred ceremonial dances, horse painting, and more.

The festival is held every year the third weekend in August, Friday from noon to 8:00 P.M., Saturday from 9:00 A.M. to 8:00 P.M., and Sunday from 9:00 A.M. to 6:00 P.M. Adult admission is $6.00; children ages six through twelve pay $4.00; children under five are free. For information, call 282–1404.

IVORYTON

Officially a section of the town of Essex, this little village is the home of the **Ivoryton Playhouse,** which since 1930 has been home to some of Connecticut's best repertory and summer stock theater companies. Now the residence of both amateur and professional groups, such as the River Rep, the theater is the site of a terrific summer series for children and the home base of one of the nation's most remarkable theater productions.

The former series is produced each Friday at 11:00 A.M. from late June through late August. Perfect for youngsters ages two to ten, it includes hour-long retellings of fairy tales, magic shows, modern classics like *You're a Good Man, Charlie Brown,* and so on. Tickets are $5.00 for both children and adults. For information, call the box office at 767–8348.

The latter productions represent the efforts of Terry Borton, owner and lead performer of the nation's one-of-a-kind **American Magic Lantern Theater.** Showman extraordinaire. and former editor-in-chief of *Weekly Reader,* the children's publication, Borton devotes his time to preserving the Victorian multimedia dramatic art that centers upon the use of a magic lantern. The amazing century-old contraption projects the images of hand-painted glass slides onto a screen while performers, including Borton, tell the tales associated with each picture.

Current performances are seasonal in nature; Halloween, Christmas, and Valentine shows are presented on the weekend prior to the three holidays. The stories and music that accompany each set of slides are taken from classic Victorian literature. Edgar Allen Poe's *The Raven,* Oliver Wendell Holmes's *The Specter Pig,* Charles Dickens's *A Christmas Carol,* Hans Christian Anderson's *The Little Match Girl,* and Longfellow's *Evangeline* and *The Love of Hiawatha* are among the eight to ten pieces of literature featured at each show.

The slides change every thirty seconds or so, and Borton's fluid manipulation produces special effects either ghastly or delightful, but always surprising. Audience participation is a large part of the magic that this marvelous three-person company creates. You help out with sound effects, you sing, and you are otherwise enthralled, enchanted, and totally engaged in this captivating performance. The shows are recommended for adults of all ages and children ages six and older.

Be sure to call prior to the three holidays to reserve seats at these often-full-house performances. Shows are presented Thursday through Saturday at 2:30 and 8:00 P.M. and Sunday at 2:30 P.M. Adult admission is $10.00; children pay $5.00. For reservations and information, call 767–5041.

MIDDLEFIELD

I mean no disrespect at all when I say that Middlefield is very aptly named. Situated north of Durham close to the New Haven County line, it is an area of fields and farms, the pretty Coginchaug River, and parts of the Cockaponset State Forest. Along with these features are three attractions particularly suited to families.

The first is **Lyman Orchards** at Routes 147 and 157. A family-owned operation since 1741, it includes apple, peach, and pear orchards, strawberry and pumpkin fields, raspberry and blueberry patches, an eighteen-hole golf course, an American-fare restaurant, and a farm store. A grand destination in every season, the farm is very popular with families wanting to pick their own produce and see the countryside.

Many festival-style events are planned throughout the year, beginning in February with a Winterfest that celebrates maple syrup season. Come here again for the Strawberry Jamboree in June, the Peach Festival in August, Apple Harvest Days in September, Pumpkin Harvest Days in October, the Apple Pie Contest in November, and visits from Santa at Christmastime. Special events such as barbecues, hayrides, or horsedrawn wagon rides are planned on festival days. The Apple Barrel Farm Store is filled daily to the brim with fresh produce and baked goods, cheeses, maple products, fudge, apple cider, and much more.

Come any time to enjoy the ducks on the pond and the clean air and sunshine. For pick-your-own updates, call 349–1566; for other information, call 349–1793.

Not far from Lyman Orchard is **Wadsworth Falls State Park** on Route 157. Typical of state parks, it has hiking trails and picnic areas, but its special attraction is a swimming area, which is available for ice-skating in the winter, and a beautiful waterfall with an overlook. One of the prettiest cascades in the state, Wadsworth Falls is a great place to spend a country afternoon. The swimming area and the falls are separate. Ask rangers or follow trails to the falls. The park is open at no charge daily year-round from 8:00 A.M. to sunset. For information, call 566–2304.

Families toying with the idea of learning to ski should fret no more over the decision. Close to home and offering a wide variety of ski school packages, the **Powder Ridge Ski Area** at 99 Powder Hill Road off Route 147 bills itself as "the place where New England learns how to ski." Specializing in children's lessons, the ski school also caters to beginner and novice adults. Even if you know your stuff, it's a great spur-of-the-moment Friday night destination that saves you the trip all the way to Vermont.

Parents and kids will love the child-centered lessons that can be done with an instructor alone or with Mom and Dad interacting as well. Skill stations allow kids to learn at their own pace and keep frustration at a minimum. Lessons are offered for children ages four and up.

Fourteen trails, five lifts, a snow-boarding area, a slopeside restaurant, and a lodge with cafeteria are all part of the facility. State-of-the-art grooming and snow-making equipment keep the slopes in optimum condition all winter long regardless of Mother Nature's cooperation. In the summer, you can use the grounds as a park, and in the fall, the lifts open for foliage rides. For information, call 349–3454.

PORTLAND

Portland has the distinction of being one of the best places from which families can view one of Connecticut's neatest river-related festivities. Held annually for more than twenty years, usually on the first Saturday in August but sometimes the last Saturday of July, this event is the **Connecticut River Raft Race.** The oldest and largest race of its kind, in Connecticut at least, it leaves from a private sandy-beach launch site in Rocky Hill and finishes at the Portland Fairgrounds off Route 17.

Held in check by some serious safety rules and regulations, the race is serious fun and the watercraft are works of art. Ranging in size from 4 by 8 feet to 12 by 36 feet, all the rafts are homemade. All participants are vying for prizes for best design, best costumes, best space craft, and so on. Individuals, associations, corporations—even the Coast Guard—participate, and all proceeds are donated to charity. The race ends roughly at the fairgrounds. Music, dancing, food concessions, clowns, and the awarding of prizes are all part of the post-race excitement.

Better than the party, though, is the fun of watching these wild and wonderful constructions come downriver. Some of these creations are two and three stories high, and each one you see will be wackier or prettier than the last. Call the numbers below for launch-time information, which can vary due to weather, and for advice as to the best viewing spots. If the race continues to finish near the fairgrounds, you'll have good viewing sites there, but check that the site hasn't changed—in years past, it's been farther downriver. Call organizers Eric Maddox (458–6025) or Daniel Jones (388–2855).

Portland is also the site of **Prehistoric Golf,** which falls squarely into the "what will they think of next" category of revived entertainments. The miniature golf industry needed a shot in the arm, and this is just what the doctor ordered. Lots of dinos are stalking the grounds of this Jurassic Park on Route 66. Don't write to me if I'm wrong about the period. All I know is that these reptiles are really big, pretty realistic, and a huge hit with mini–miniature golfers.

No more windmills here, folks. Just tropical-looking vegetation, waterfalls, and towering beasts. They light the place up at night to encourage you to play another round. Group and birthday party discounts are offered. The course is open daily from 10:00 A.M. to 10:30 P.M. On summer Fridays and Saturdays, it stays open until 11:00 P.M. Call to inquire about the playing season; it varies according to the weather and how many people seem to be interested. For information, call 342–3517.

WESTBROOK/OLD SAYBROOK/CLINTON

These towns comprise Middlesex County's trio of Long Island Sound shoreline towns. Easy to group together because of their geography, they are also similar in other ways. These are the towns where you eat crab-cakes and clam strips and play real mini-golf with windmills and light-houses. Where you stroll along seawalls, have double-dip ice cream cones, and skip stones off the jetty. Where you walk barefoot and break out in freckles and let the sun bleach your hair. These are the towns of summer.

Very, very low in true "suck-'em-in" tourist attractions, you can wander for hours along the shore roads that splinter south from the Boston Post Road. Also known as Route 1, footpath of the Pequot Indians and stomping grounds of the Connecticut beach bums, this road is richer than a sea captain's treasure chest. Seafood shacks, antiques shops, ice-cream parlors, and all that sort of half-rundown Cape Cod–y kind of emporiums are designed to make you put on your browsing shoes.

Make your first stop Saybrook Point. It is here that nature provided the Connecticut River Valley her first big break. Down near the mouth of the river, there's a big old sandbar that prevents huge oceangoing vessels from entering the river. Thanks to the sandbar, which makes the Connecticut the largest river in America without a port, the river has stayed healthier than many others and her towns have retained many of their old-time characteristics.

Follow Route 154 from Route 1 to the Point. Stop on your way at the **James Pharmacy and Soda Fountain** at 2 Pennywise Lane, which is really right there at the edge of Route 154. Built in 1790 as the general store for the historic Pratt Tavern, this white clapboarded building with the red and white awnings has operated as a pharmacy from 1877 to 1994. Originally owned by Peter Lane, the business was turned over to Miss Ana Louise James in 1917. The first black woman pharmacist in Connecticut, the well-loved Miss James ran the store for fifty years, and it is being operated now by Kim and Garth Meadows.

The pharmacy contains all of its original wooden display cases and fixtures, a 1905 oak phone booth (which works), and an 1896 soda fountain complete with a huge gray marble bar, oak "Coke" tables and chairs, and old black and white floor tiles. You can buy everything from aspirin to yo-yos in the pharmacy/general store, but it is in the soda fountain that the real pull on your willpower begins.

How about a slice of sour cream coffeecake and an iced cappuccino? Or a dip into one of those glass jars filled with fireballs and jelly beans? An old-fashioned New York–style egg cream? How about a two-scoop milk-shake spun fresh on the Hamilton Beach, reputed to be "the best in the world"?

Take it from us—the very best deal is the Big Bri's Turtle Tickler. This concoction is made from turtle ice cream, which is vanilla with caramel, pecans, and chocolate pieces—draped with hot butterscotch, crowned with whipped cream, and laced with chocolate syrup. It's to die for—in fact, don't get your cholesterol tested for at least a week after sampling this one. Break loose, have a ball—my Aunt Ruth said one of these once in a while won't hurt you, and she's a pediatrician. For information, call 388–2566.

Continue down to the Point and stroll there for a while. Heavy with salt and briny mud aromas of the sea and shore and marsh, the air here carries the sounds of screeching gulls, slapping rigging, lonesome train whistles, and bellowing foghorns.You can see the breakwater that protects the harbor and you can watch the boats and gulls and swans. **Saybrook Point Mini-Golf Course** (388–2407) is one of the best around here, and there is not an African mammal or Jurassic reptile in sight—just Flipper the Seal, the Eiffel Tower, Ye Olde Mill, and the Wishing Pond near the Brooklyn Bridge. You know—*normal* mini-golf.

You can pick up a bite to eat at the **Dock & Dine** Quick Bites Gazebo, and you can see the artwork of the **Saybrook Colony Artists** at their gallery on the walkway near the river. Then get back in the car and follow Route 154 around the peninsula (you'll turn left shortly after you leave the Point parking lot—don't head back toward town). When you arrive at Route 1, turn left and drive toward Westbrook.

You'll have a real dilemma soon if you're hungry for lunch or dinner. You can stop in Old Saybrook at 1654 Boston Post Road for the best pizza made anywhere between Providence and New Haven or you can hold out until you reach the seafood king at the Singing Bridge in Westbrook.

Alforno Brick Oven Pizzeria and Ristorante is, in our opinion, the only place to go to eat pizza on the shoreline. Thin, crisp, crust, fresh toppings, excellent sauce, great salads, good pasta, and more are on the menu. Children love to watch their own pizza being created before their eyes on the marble counter. Expert tossing of the dough makes for a thin, yet tender crust, and the 610-degree brick oven bakes it to perfection in six to eight minutes. If you can wait for a table, you won't be disappointed. For information, call 399–4166.

If seafood wins the toss of the coin, go straight to **Bill's Seafood Restaurant** at the Singing Bridge in Westbrook (399–7224). You can't miss it. You'll cross the metal deck of the steel bridge and to your right is the conglomeration of structures known as Bill's. This is by no means the only seafood shack on Route 1 and it may not even be the best, but it's our favorite for a few reasons. The food is good, the prices are reasonable, and the setting couldn't be more picturesque. The kids like to feed the ducks that hang out near the riverside deck, there's a lighted Christmas tree out on the riverbank all summer long, and the bridge *does* sing. The moon rises nicely over the boats in the marina, and the clientele is much more colorful and interesting than in fancier places. So, if you're going to eat chowder and steamers and clam strips, you might as well do it here.

After you eat, drive back along the Boston Post Road and turn right onto Seaview Avenue. Offering one of the prettiest views of the water and the offshore islands, this route takes you past the **Westbrook Town Beach** where, for a small day fee non-residents pay only in summer, you can spend the day on the sand or stroll the long seawalk. This very clean beach is great for young children. Its swimming area has an extraordinarily sandy bottom that slopes very gradually toward deeper water.

Continue toward Clinton by driving west on Route 1. It too has pretty views of the water from its beach roads and a variety of restaurants, antiques shops, and ice-cream emporiums perfect for whiling away a summer afternoon. Visitors can use the **Clinton Town Beach** for a small day fee; it's at the end of Waterside Lane off Route 1. Cross the bridge at the foot of the road and enter the beach area. A playground, restrooms, and a seasonal snack bar are here.

Last in Middlesex County is a little bit of magic before you head home. Best seen in the twilight when the air is crisp and your breath rises steamily from your throat, **The Pink Sleigh** (399–6926) on Route 153 in Westbrook is a haven of peace for anyone who delights in the wonder of Christmas. This store is beautiful—a place where every small child will suck in his or her breath in awe of its glitter and gold. Dazzling displays of every color and material fill the two-story rustic barn, which in itself is beautiful. Stepping into this place on an autumn afternoon just as twilight falls is like coming upon an elfin workshop hidden in the hills. I know it's a store, but it fills the heart with hope. Open from early July until Christmas Eve, Tuesday through Friday from 10:00 A.M. to 5:00 P.M.

TOLLAND COUNTY

The hills of northeastern Connecticut have magic in them. As with Washington Irving's Catskills, something within these knolls has defied the physical laws governing the passage of time. The traveler is transported centuries backward just by being here. This is not a place well known for action. The magic of Tolland County lies not in what one *does* here. Rather, its magic lies partly in the sweet relief of having nothing to do here. It is, simply, a nice place just to be.

Families looking for the quieter pleasures of life in New England will find much to please them here. The museums are smaller and have fewer buttons to press, but they are no less excellent than their showy counterparts in the city. The activities have fewer moving parts and use little or no fossil fuel, but they'll invigorate the body, feed the soul, and leave time for the mind to restore itself.

COVENTRY

Coventry is one of our favorite Connecticut towns. Neatly in the middle of the southern end of the county, its rolling woodlands are laced with mile upon mile of twisting country roads, beautiful in every season.

Like many of the towns in the area, Coventry's chief temptations are its scenic byways, farmstands, antiques shops, and inns. The slick stuff of the city is not to be found here. Still, Coventry provides a trio of attractions

Somers

84

44 Storrs

Mansfield

Coventry

Tolland County

that will appeal to any family that enjoys history or nature—or toys.

Stop first at the home of Connecticut's state hero, Nathan Hale. At 2299 South Street on the fringe of the Nathan Hale State Forest off Route 31, the **Nathan Hale Homestead** is perhaps the most stately of Revolutionary War–era historic homes in the country. Its site on the property is a fitting memorial to the proud young man who lost his life in the service of his country in September 1776.

Nathan never actually lived in the house currently standing on his family's farm. While he was serving in the Continental Army, the house was being built to replace the smaller house in which Nathan and his eleven siblings had been raised. Sometime after the death of the first Mrs. Hale (I presume from exhaustion), Nathan's father, Deacon Richard Hale, married the second Mrs. Hale, a widow with seven children of her own. Clearly there was just cause for building a new homestead. Sadly, Nathan never saw the house that represented not only breathing space but the prosperity that his father had achieved in their new, beloved land. His family moved into the new house just a month after his death.

At twenty-one years of age, Nathan, a graduate of the class of 1773 at Yale and a teacher by profession, set out on the most dangerous mission known to his generation. Acting under the principles of freedom that drove the Patriot cause, Nathan, now a captain in the rebel army, walked on foot in the disguise of a poor schoolmaster to infiltrate the British encampment at New York City and bring the plans of the enemy back to General Washington. Apprehended within sight of the smoke from the American campfires, Nathan was relieved of the secrets he had written on a parchment hidden in his boot and was hung from the gallows without a trial.

It was on this occasion, facing his death, that Nathan Hale uttered his most famous words: "I only regret that I have but one life to lose for my country." His body was left hanging for three days as a warning to other traitors and was buried in an unmarked grave in Artillery Field, now underneath the pavement near Manhattan's Sixty-sixth Street and Third Avenue.

The homestead tour includes the grounds and the house. It begins with an excellent short film shown in the small outbuilding to the left of the house. The house includes many Hale furnishings and belongings, including Nathan's musket, his shoe buckles, the trunk he left with his friend Asher Wright when he left on his mission, and the Bible he recieved as a gift on his seventeenth birthday. The tours are among the best for children we have heard in the state—filled with detail but quick and not above the heads of young listeners. The tours are given every half-hour from 1:00 to 5:00 P.M. daily from May 15 to October 15.

In addition, several special days are planned annually. On Mother's Day the two Mrs. Hales appear to portray motherhood in the eighteenth century, and mothers are admitted at no charge. In early June, Nathan's birthday is celebrated with cake, special tours, and a performance by the Nathan Hale Ancient Fife and Drum Corps. In mid-July, an Antiques Festival with one hundred or more exhibitors and refreshments accompanies the tours. In late July, a Revolutionary War encampment takes over the grounds for a full weekend of camp-life reenactments and a multicorps fife and drum muster. In late September a mourning day commemorates Nathan's death with special events and tours. Lastly, in late October (but never exactly on Halloween night) a lantern light tour of the property begins down the street at the Strong-Porter House and proceeds along the

The interpretive guides at the Nathanial Hale Homestead will make a trip there both educatonal and fun. (Courtesy Antiquarian and Landmarks Society/Nathanial Hale Homestead)

road to the Hale Homestead, where several individuals portray events of the ghostly past. Who knows what might happen on a late October night in New England? This last event has been a sell-out for the past five years.

On an ordinary day, admission for adults is $4.00; children are charged $1.00. Special days involve no extra charge, except for the October lantern light festivities. The staff here also run an exceptionally good Colonial Life Camp for middle-school children. A week-long day camp, it involves kids in colonial games, crafts, weaving, cooking, clothes-making, plant study, and the opportunity to role-play a Hale historical character. The camp is often a sell-out; many kids travel from other parts of the state to participate. For information, call 742–6917 or 247–8996.

When you leave the Homestead, bear to the left on South Street and drive down the road a piece until you reach Silver Road on your right. About a half-mile up on your left at 534 Silver Road is **Caprilands,** a haven of fragrance and loveliness hidden in the woodlands but open to all the world. The empire of reigning herb queen Adelma Grenier Simmons, the fifty-acre herb farm is especially appealing to children who have read Frances Hodgson Burnett's *The Secret Garden.* In every corner of the property is a themed garden of one sort or another, most with poetic names that conjure up romantic images and make one half expect to meet some mythical creature along the pretty paths.

If you are lucky, you will meet the queen herself. Ms. Adelma Simmons is quite a lady—a lady, by the way, who never reveals her age, though she'll tell you that she has been at her craft since 1929. Her handiwork, creativity, and wholesome spirit of celebration are everywhere apparent at Caprilands. Knowledgeable and enthusiastic about every aspect of herb gardening, Ms. Simmons will send you home with hope and advice and excellent plants to get you going. If the kids aren't thrown by her somewhat eccentric appearance (her clothes are of a fanciful vintage nature, and she is, of course, a very old woman), they will enjoy meeting her, too. Her zest for living is an inspiration, and her love of all living things extends to small critters of the human variety as well as the botanical.

In addition to thirty-eight themed gardens and a book shop, you will find a basket shop, a large barn loaded with garden-related gifts, and greenhouses brimming with plants for sale. You can visit Ms. Simmons's eighteenth-century home on the property, too. Its downstairs is a lovely luncheon space, draped from every rafter with dried specimens of the gardens. Herbal luncheons are given here Monday through Saturday at noon from April through October, but these are not children's affairs. Each five-course luncheon features foods prepared with fresh herbs, sauces, and vinegars made at Caprilands and is followed by a lecture and a tour of the gardens.

The grounds are most lush in late spring and throughout summer, with some raggedy edges showing by late autumn and dormancy in winter; Caprilands nevertheless is open year-round. Christmas is what Adelma calls the fifth season of the year. No matter how bare the gardens look in December, the greenhouses and barn are alive with the magic she cultivates. Come unannounced anytime daily from 9:00 A.M. to 5:00 P.M. For luncheons or for the high tea served Sundays at 2:00 p.m., you must make reservations. Admission to the gardens is free. Luncheons are $18.00 per adult; teas are $12.00. For reservations or information, call 742–7244.

Not far from these places at 41 North River Road directly off Route 31 is the **Special Joys Doll and Toy Museum** (and store and bed and breakfast). The small museum of high-quality, tastefully displayed collectible and antique dolls and toys includes such treasures as Steiff, Jumeau, Kathe Kruse, and Shuco dolls and animals. A few of these are animated; all are beautiful. Many of the dolls are placed among unusual pieces of antique or collectible doll furnishings, carefully arranged to illustrate room settings of the period most closely related to the era of the dolls themselves. Small and rare accessories are displayed along with the furniture. You can purchase items for sale in the shop next to the museum, and if you have something special you want to sell or get an opinion on, you can bring it along with you. The museum and shop are open year-round Wednesday through Sunday from 11:00 A.M. to 5:00 P.M. Admission is free.

If the day's activities have worn you plumb out, you might want to set a spell at the Special Joys pink-towered Victorian bed and breakfast. They have three air-conditioned guest rooms (two with private bath), and they'll provide televisions if you really want to spoil the ambience. Children are very welcome, but smoking and pets are taboo. A full country-style breakfast will jump-start the whole gang for another day of family fun. For reservations or information, call 742–6359.

MANSFIELD

If you don't have a grip on the township concept, you'll have a chance to study it fully in Mansfield. Comprised of several village centers and a large university, Mansfield lies roughly between Routes 44 and 6 at the north and south, respectively, and is crisscrossed by Routes 195, 275, 32, and 89.

I mention this because even if you have driven for miles you will know that you are still in Mansfield if you are between any of these points, a fact that can become very important since the village names are Mansfield Depot, Mansfield Center, and Mansfield Four Corners—and also Eagleville, Spring Hill, and Storrs (which is the home of the University of Connecticut and the name by which most out-of-towners refer to Mansfield). For the purposes of this book, we are going to group the university-related attractions under the town heading of Storrs just a few pages onward (see page 133).

Start a day in Mansfield at **Mansfield Hollow State Park** just about a mile east of Mansfield Center near the junction of Routes 195 and 89. Created to protect the land around the 500-acre reservoir manufactured by the damming of the Natchaug River by the Army Corps of Engineers, the park includes more than 2,000 acres of open space perfect for hiking, picnicking, cross-country skiing, and bird- or wildlife-watching.

Among the amenities are a field sports area, a picnic grove (with tall pine trees, tables, firepits, restrooms, and seasonal water fountains), horseshoe pits, an interpretive nature trail, and miles of other hiking trails. Unfortunately, because the lake is a public water supply, you can't swim here, but you can bring in your fossil-fuel-burning powerboat at the public boat launch. As they say in New York, go figure. You can also fish. I guess the fish don't mind the petrochemicals.

Follow the signs to the 1952 Mansfield Dam (you can walk to it along the top of the dike that runs through the first part of the park or you can drive to it on the roads). The dam is a fairly impressive structure (unless you've already seen Hoover, of course), and it overlooks the lake, the river, and Kirby Mill, a stone structure dating from 1882. Tours of the dam are given periodically; call the number below for a schedule. The park is open year-round from sunrise to sunset. Trash containers are not provided, so be prepared. The park is an alcohol-free facility, so leave the wine and beer out of your picnic fixings. Admission is free. Call 455–9057.

For fun in a time warp, stay until evening for one of the first-run films playing at the **Mansfield Drive-In Theater.** If you were a child of the 1950s or 1960s, you probably know how this works: The kids get into pajamas just before dark and pile into the Ford Country Squire, and the whole family cheerfully heads off to the drive-in to watch wholesome, family-values-type movies under the stars.

If it's really warm, the kids spread a blanket on the roof of the car and pile on top, hoping to get a good view of anything interesting going on in the next car. There's lots of giggling involved and lots of popcorn, and when there's too much noise on the roof, Dad says something like "June, can you make those kids settle down?" and Mom says something like,"Oh, Ward, they're just high-spirited," and everybody starts giggling again.

Today the Mansfield Drive-In is one of only three drive-ins remaining in Connecticut and the only one east of the Connecticut River. The Mansfield's three screens offer "family" films, but call to be sure you share their opinion of appropriate films for your children. They are open Friday through Sunday evening in April, May, and September and every night in June, July, and August. Wednesday night is Family Night, which means a special per-carload price. During the most recent season, you could load up the mini-van and take the whole gang to the movies for $6.50. For information, call 423–4441.

SOMERS

Way up north in Tolland County, just a stone's throw from the Massachusetts border, is the small town of Somers, pronounced like the season. Not far from the town center at the junction of Routes 83 and 190 is the **Somers Mountain Indian Museum** at 332 Turnpike Road. Dedicated to the idea that all humans can learn to live in harmony with the earth and with each other, this museum is a proud and touching reminder of the legacy of the Native American people.

Its vast collection of artifacts has been gathered from all parts of North America. Arrowheads, buckskin clothing and bags, war clubs, moccasins, masks, baskets, jewelry, pottery, rugs, pipes, and tools are among the thousands of items from the Pacific Northwest coast, the Southwest, the Eastern Woodlands, and the Great Plains. Mostly acquired through the efforts of the museum's founder, James F. King, the collection also includes artifacts from the American Revolution, the French and Indian Wars, the Civil War, and the eighteenth-century whaling industry.

The museum is open year-round except for January, Wednesday through Saturday from 10:00 A.M. to 5:00 P.M. and Sunday from 11:00 A.M. to 5:00 P.M. The staff is very willing to share their knowledge of the collection and of Native American culture and history in general. Programs are offered from time to time; hands-on activities such as flint-knapping or bow-making could be on the docket during one of your visits.

A small gift shop offers books, bird feeders, Native American music, Southwestern jewelry, and other works from local craftspeople. A picnic area on the grounds gives families the opportunity to rest awhile in this vernal setting; you are also welcome to explore the nature trails on the property. Admission to the museum is $2.00 for adults and 99 cents for children over five. For information, call 749–4129.

If you are in the area in late June, come for the **Annual Strawberry Moon Powwow** held at the Four Town Fairgrounds on Eygpt Road. Traditionally the Indian time of forgiveness and healing, the Strawberry Moon festival features storytelling, children's dancing and games, traditional drums, arts and crafts, educational demonstrations, and native foods. Held from 11:00 A.M. to 7:00 P.M. on Saturday and Sunday of the last weekend in June, the festival asks for $5.00 per adult visitor and $3.00 for children six through twelve. For information, call 684–6984.

STORRS

Not surprisingly, the University of Connecticut provides several resources for family adventure on its main campus at Storrs. The first is the **Connecticut State Museum of Natural History.** Its permanent collection includes more than two million artifacts, but space doesn't allow them to astound visitors with all of these at once. Currently, the museum has three separate areas with permanent and/or changing exhibits.

The first area is the Shark Exhibit in the Jorgensen Auditorium. Photographs and text explore the facts and mysteries of shark biology and reproduction, their feeding habits, and their life cycle. A fiberglass reproduction of the largest shark ever caught in New England waters is also here. Taken just off the shore of Block Island in 1983, the thirty-two- to forty-three-year-old giant is 7 feet tall, 15 feet long, and weighs 2,779 pounds. The fiberglass model is fitted with the shark's real teeth. Enter the Jorgensen Building through the Nutmeg Entrance and follow the signs to the exhibit. It is open weekdays from 8:00 A.M. to 4:00 P.M.

The second area in the museum includes the Biology Greenhouses, which house the most diverse collection of plants between New York and Boston. Nearly 4,000 species thrive here, including more than 500 species of orchids. This may be the closest you come to a rainforest—it's lush and humid and lovely. The greenhouses are outside the Torrey Life Sciences Building. Come during the week anytime from 8:00 A.M. to 4:00 P.M.

The third area is the main exhibit space that features both permanent and changing displays from the museum's collection. Exhibited on a rotating basis, the collection includes a fascinating array of human artifacts and animal specimens superbly arranged for visitors of all ages.

The excellent cornerstone of the exhibit is *One Circle Home: Life in an Algonkian Indian Culture.* A small but life-sized bark wigwam is the centerpiece of the display. Fully equipped with all the furnishings typical of a pre-European Algonkian roundhouse, it provides a realistic look at the lifestyle and belief system of the Algonkian people. Hands-on activities encircling the base of the wigwam model explain the games, instruments, and tools of the culture. The dignity and spirituality of the people are portrayed remarkably well in this minimalist, earth-toned exhibit.

Nearby is a small aquarium with field guides available to help visitors identify the creatures within the tank. Next to that is the wonderful Eugene Allen collection of mounted raptors of North America, which includes the beautiful owls and hawks of New England. We recently saw an exhibit of neotropical butterflies, a collection of hand-carved Zuni hunting fetishes, one case of beaded Native American moccasins and another of Peruvian pottery, a photographic display of the amazing blue-footed booby bird, and a collection of grass baskets. If you were to visit several times yearly, you would find new exhibits each time.

The museum's most famous attraction is **Videoplace,** an interactive, hand-wired computer-activated artificial reality extravaganza. The brainchild of Dr. Myron Krueger, Videoplace may not impress you initially.

Situated in a somewhat small space, it is at first glance nothing more than a large back-lit screen juxtaposed with a large-screen monitor in front of which rests some video equipment of rather discreet proportions. But when you step between the back-lit screen and the monitor, the magic starts.

An ever-increasing number (currently about twenty-four) of games or interactions can be explored, each for as long as you remain between the back-lit screen and the monitor. Basically, the computer plays a game that you control with your movements. You can make the colors of the rainbow follow the moving silhouette of your body; you can cause the sun to set over the Manhattan skyline and then you can turn on all the lights in the skyscrapers; you can draw with your fingertip; or you can hunt down and capture the mischievous Critter before it dances its victory jig on the top of your head. You can even play Cat's Cradle or make colorful Angels-in-the-Snow.

Dr. Krueger's award-winning and world-famous creation is sometimes on display out of the state or country, so if you're headed to UConn specifically to see this exhibit, call the number below first to find out if it's at home. Just a bit of advice: Videoplace works best with just one or two people at a time. My oldest daughter was quite frustrated with the antics of her sisters, but when she had some time one-on-one with the computer, I had to drag her out of there by the elbow an hour later.

This main exhibit area of the museum is housed in just one large room in the gold-domed Wilbur Cross Building. It just may have to expand soon, since the staff are putting the finishing touches on a brand-new, one-of-a-kind, very slick and sophisticated interactive shark exhibit with tremendous kid-appeal. The Wilbur Cross Exhibit Room is open year-round Monday, Thursday, Friday, and Saturday from noon to 4:00 P.M. and Sunday from 1:00 to 4:00 P.M.

Admission to all areas of the museum is free, though donations are gratefully accepted. Of special interest to families are the four to six Family Days arranged each year. These programs are held from 1:00 to 5:00 P.M. on weekends throughout the spring and summer; some programs are two-day affairs. They are free to members of the museum, UConn students, members of the local chapter of the Audubon Society, and children under five. Other adults pay $5.00, and children five through seventeen pay $2.00. The shows feature hands-on science and arts-and-crafts activities for children, slide talks by experts, living plant or animal exhibits and demonstrations, and refreshments.

The Live Reptile and Amphibian Show is perhaps the largest such event in the United States. The Live Insect Show is certainly the largest such program east of the Mississippi. You can also see the Live Birds Show, the Wildflower Festival, and the popular Our Dynamic Earth Show. In mid-November, the Connecticut Archaeology Family Day offers lectures by experts, continuous hands-on activities for children, exhibits of pre-Colonial and eighteenth- and nineteenth-century artifacts, and demonstrations of Native American arts and crafts. For more information on the museum and its special events, call 486–4460.

Just across the courtyard behind the Wilbur Cross Building is the **William Benton Museum of Art.** Currently, just two galleries are devoted to changing exhibitions and displays from the 3,000–piece permanent collection. Admission is free here also, and the size of the museum makes it a wonderful place in which to introduce children to fine art. The museum's exhibitions are of the highest caliber. While directed mostly at adult visitors and students of fine art, some are of great appeal to children. A recent summer's exhibition of 200 marionettes, glove puppets, rod puppets, and shadow puppets was introduced by a musical parade of dancers, lantern carriers, peacocks, and a royal white elephant. For information, call 486–3530.

The university also has a fairly well-kept secret in its School of Agriculture. At the **Dairy Barn** just a ways north of Gurleyville Road on Route 195, you can buy ice cream freshly made, year-round, by students. The ice cream is sensational, the price is lower than average, and the portions are enormous. In season, the peach ice cream is pure bliss. One of my daughters would argue that raspberry cheesecake is the way to go, but the flavors change all the time—after all, these are creative college kids. Don't be thrown by the clinical look of this facility; it is not by any means an ice-cream parlor. Just wait until you taste the product—you won't need any fancy window trimmings. It is open Monday through Friday from 10:00 A.M. to 5:00 P.M. and on Saturday and Sunday from noon to 5:00 P.M. It closes on major holidays. Call 486–3530.

WINDHAM COUNTY

I don't know when some clever copywriter labeled Tolland and Windham counties the "Quiet Corner," but the name has stuck so thoroughly that you might think it is the official name of the region. Though Tolland County shares the name, it is here in Windham that the full impact of the term hits the traveler. *It's quiet here.*

Although a portion of the county is sliced by I–395, which leads travelers toward Worcester, Boston, and points beyond, the county is little altered by the traffic. In fact, the proprietors of its museums, shops, and inns have deliberately and successfully maintained the regions old-fashioned ambience, partly to please those very travelers.

Families looking for adventure in Windham County are going to find mostly simple pleasures. Kick back, take your shoes off, sit a spell. Get ready to use your senses. This is a place to explore, to take a deep breath, to listen to the brooks, the breezes, and the birds. It's a place to contemplate how this land—all of this land, this whole now–United States—must have looked before 1636 when European settlers arrived bringing vast changes to the native civilization.

BALLOUVILLE

Neither the seventeeth-century Algonkian people nor the colonial settlers would have had any means by which to process the magic of Mr. Merwin

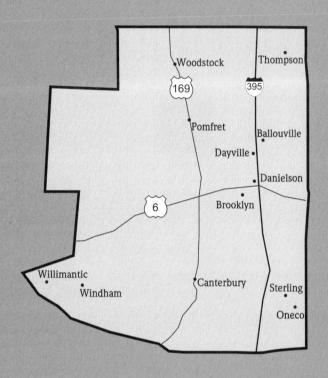

Woodstock
Thompson

(169) (395)

Pomfret
Ballouville

Dayville

Danielson

Brooklyn
(6)

Willimantic
Windham
Canterbury
Sterling
Oneco

Windham County

Whipple of Ballouville—that I can guarantee. Every year for the past twenty-seven, Mr. Whipple has produced a Christmas extravaganza the likes of which I have never seen before. The Disney Main Street Electrical Parade might be a close runner-up, but you ought to see this phenomenon first before making any judgments. It's incredible.

The **Christmas Wonderland** at 101 Pineville Road is just 2¼ miles from exit 94 off I–395. Follow the signs from the highway and prepare to be dumbstruck. Mr. Whipple's personal tribute to the glory and magic of Christmas spreads throughout his property. A twelve-building miniature village, six display buildings, a granite chapel, and a showroom nearly as big as my house are illuminated by 100,000 twinkling lights. All of these areas are animated by 350 moving displays and Christmas characters.

Inside and out, the spectacular scene is enough to overwhelm even the grumpiest of Scrooges. If you are too tired from the labors of Thanksgiving festivities to even think about Christmas, come here for the jolt you might need to remember the awesome meaning of the holiday. If the spirit of Christmas doesn't possess you here, it won't overtake you anywhere.

In recent years about 50,000 visitors have come to see this fantasy-land of elves, reindeer, Wise Kings, shepherds, polar inhabitants, and so much more. Music of the season plays continuously, filling the ears with holiday messages the eyes may have missed. Each evening, including Christmas Eve, Santa greets every child who wants to see him and gives a small gift to each and every one.

Everything here is free, unless you care to make a donation or buy a postcard, but Mr. Whipple isn't asking for a penny. His $4,000 electrical bill each season has done nothing to diminish his generous spirit. In fact, Mr. Whipple has a flair for making people happy. A Justice of the Peace, he has officiated at 1,600 weddings in his little granite chapel.

The Wonderland opens Thanksgiving weekend and closes at 10:00 p.m New Year's Day. Every evening, the lights are turned on at 5:00 P.M. Santa goes home to rest each night at 9:00 but the lights, action, and music continue until 10:00 P.M. For information, call 774–2742.

BROOKLYN

Windham County contains one of the top ten scenic highways in the

United States, selected for that distinction by Scenic America, an environ-
mental organization that works, in part, to identify and protect scenic
American roads. Historically known as the Norwich–Woodstock Turnpike,
the 32-mile section of Route 169 that lies between Taftville, just north of
Norwich, and Woodstock is just about as pretty as pretty can get. Part of
that route goes through Brooklyn, a quaint village with beautiful New
England churches and a monument to Revolutionary War hero General
Israel Putnam in its center.

Every year in late August, Brooklyn's population soars as visitors from
all over come to the oldest continuously active agricultural fair in the
United States. Held for four days the weekend before Labor Day, the
Brooklyn Fair is perhaps the best country fair in the state. Just name the
activities and sights you expect at a country fair—you'll find them all here.

Here's a partial list of what's in store for you: Oxen Pull. Draft Horse
Show. Skillet Toss. Dog Show. Circus. Midway. Petting Zoo. Baking
Contest. Pony Pull. Cattle Parade. Christmas Tree Show. Livestock
Demonstrations. Bingo. Barbecue. Antique Tractor Pull. Country Music.
Dancing. Bee-keeping Exhibit. Children's Games and Contests. Art Show.
Stage Entertainment for Adults and Children.

The list goes on and on. Of course, the printed word cannot capture
the diversity of sounds, smells, and sights that assault the senses at a fair of
this sort, but I can assure you that your kids are going to love this event.
Children under twelve are admitted at no charge; adults pay $2.00 on
Thursday evening, $4.00 on Friday, and $5.00 on Saturday and Sunday.
Parking is an additional $2.00 per car.

Don't be fooled by the seemingly low admission fees. Although the
agricultural events are all free and you can look at all you want for nothing, you'll need a wad of currency for an outing here. That is unless you
and the kids don't eat any food, buy any crafts or gadgets, or go on any
rides. I suspect some families save up all year for the fair. Regardless of the
expense, this is good old-fashioned fun for the whole family.

Traditionally the fair opens on Thursday at 4:00 P.M. and closes at
11:00 P.M. On Friday, Saturday, and Sunday, it opens at 9:00 A.M. and closes at 11:00 P.M. For information, call 779–0012.

CANTERBURY

Several miles south of Brooklyn on Route 169 is Canterbury, famed for its own architectural style and for Crandall Academy, founded in 1832 by Prudence Crandall. Site of the first New England academy for black girls, the Academy is now called the **Prudence Crandall Museum.**

Located on the green at the corner of Routes 169 and 14, the 1805 structure is also one of the several houses in town with the distinctive "Canterbury style." Basically conforming to the Federal style, the house has twin chimneys and an elaborate two-story entrance ornamentation with a Palladian window on the second floor above the front doorway.

Far more famous than its architecture is the house's history and its mistress, Prudence Crandall. In the summer of 1831, twenty-eight-year-old Prudence was asked by a group of Canterbury citizens to establish a private academy in which she would teach local children. She purchased a large house on the Canterbury Green and opened her academy in January 1832. All went well for several months. Miss Crandall had the full support of the parents, who paid her twenty-five dollars per quarter to teach their children reading, writing, arithmetic, grammar, geography, history, philosophy, chemistry, and astronomy.

Then, in the fall of 1832, she accepted a new student. Sarah Harris, twenty years old, was Negro. Disapproval was immediate, and several families withdrew their children from the academy. Criticism was so harsh that Miss Crandall dismissed the remaining students and reopened the school several months later as an academy for the instruction of "young ladies and little misses of color."

The first such school in all of New England, the academy added classes in French, drawing, painting, and piano. Outrage followed the earlier criticism, as Miss Crandall made it clear that no distinctions were to be made in the education of white and black children. In May 1833, Prudence Crandall was arrested and jailed for breaking the Connecticut General Asssembly's new "Black Law," which prohibited the instruction of any "colored persons who are not inhabitants of this State."

Though her case was dismissed in July, Prudence and her students suffered greatly at the hands of the citizens of the Canterbury area. The house was pelted with rocks and eggs. An attempt was made to set it afire, and its windows were broken in an angry attack in September 1834. Only then, fearing the physical safety of her students, did she close the school.

The story of Prudence Crandall's courage and the dignity of her students is told in tours of the museum. Changing and permanent exhibits explore topics such as local history, black history, the abolitionist movement, and women's rights. The museum also includes three period rooms, a very good gift shop, and a research library.

Families might especially enjoy "Prudence Crandall Day" on the Saturday of Labor Day weekend. This special festivity offers nineteenth-century children's games, craft demonstrations, musical entertainment, and refreshments and crafts for sale. Tours of the museum on that day are directed especially to children, but regular tours are also tailored to family groups that may come daytripping.

The museum is open January 15 through December 15, Wednesday through Sunday from 10:00 A.M. to 4:30 P.M. Admission is $2.00 for adults and $1.00 for children. For information, call 546–9916.

Also in Canterbury is **Wright's Mill Tree Farm,** at 63 Creasey Road. Once the site of five seventeenth-century mills, the beautiful 250-acre property is an outstanding place to take your family. Amidst one of the prettiest New England settings I've seen, you can pick pumpkins, cut Christmas trees, walk nature trails to antique mill sites, and soak up the aura of the olden days that percolates from every pore of this refuge.

Owner Al Amundsen loves tourists and is expanding operations at Wright's Mill to please folks who have high hopes for a wonderful day in the country. He's already pleasing people left and right, and I'd argue with anyone who would disagree that this man is the sort who hasn't yet met a child he doesn't like. There's not a place on the planet where children are more welcome.

The farm is open to the public daily year-round, but the level of activity varies from season to season. Here, for instance, spring begins on April 1, when the Garden Center opens. In late April an Arbor Day celebration means a free talk for children on how to grow their own gardens, and every child receives a free seedling tree.

All summer you can explore the trails, skip stones on the pond, climb

A horse-drawn carriage ride at Wright's Mill Tree Farm is a real treat. (Courtesy Wright's Mill Tree Farm)

the spiral staircase of the silo in the Christmas Shop for a bird's-eye view of the terrain. See if any dancing is going on in the outdoor pavilion, or have a picnic anywhere you choose in these tranquil hills.

Come again in autumn for the Fall Fling Festival, Pumpkin Hunt Hayrides, Spooky Hayrides, and the Grand Arrival of Santa. The three-day fall festival on Columbus Day weekend offers a crafts show, guided nature walks, pony rides for the kids, and much more. The foliage is spectacular, and nothing will compare to a horsedrawn wagon ride through the splendidly crunchy leaves.

On a mid-October to Halloween weekend evening, take a Spooky Hayride into the dark, dark woods for a glimpse at the spirit world. Get ready to shriek and shiver. The rides run from Thursday to Saturday from 6:00 P.M. to midnight; call for age recommendations and current prices.

Perhaps it will be winter that you find most enchanting here. I am certain that there is in all New England no setting more like a Currier and Ives painting than this one. The Grand Arrival of Santa in a horsedrawn sleigh on the day after Thanksgiving heralds the opening of tree-cutting season. In the farm's thirty-one fields grow 150,000 trees in thirteen varieties; if you want to do the cutting yourself, the Amundsens provide maps, saws, and great little wooden carts for dragging in the most beautiful Christmas trees ever. You can also buy pre-cut trees, holly-studded wreaths, garlands, and so on.

Santa or one of his elves gives every child a candy cane and listens to every Christmas wishlist. The Chowdanooga Choo Choo sells hot food to warm you on the weekends; during the week, the Amundsens often provide cookies and cider or cocoa for the little ones. The Christmas Shop is brimming with ornaments; you can shop while the kids slide on the frozen pond—that is, if the weather cooperates. Come any day of the week during December from 9:00 A.M. to dark. There may be no better Christmas tree farm anywhere—come and see for yourself. Admission to the farm is free for all ages. For information, call 774–1455.

DAYVILLE

Put on your dungarees and some sturdy shoes and head up the trail to Dayville for a day or weekend of adventure at the **Diamond A Ranch.** This place is another that runs on the belief that children are very nice people. It offers guided trail rides and horseback riding lessons for all ages on the gently rolling property at 975 Hartford Turnpike. From exit 93 off I–395, drive 1 1/10 miles east on Route 101 and look for the Diamond A.

Owner Alicia Summar has created some great opportunities for families with children ages two and up to enjoy the pretty terrain of her ranch. Trail rides ranging from one-hour outings to weekend excursions are offered nearly year-round, at least as long as there is no ice on the ground. Drop-ins are welcome, but reservations are recommended. During peak foliage season, you are unlikely to find a single unreserved horse all weekend long. Rides range from $15 per person for one hour to $10 per hour per person for rides of three or more hours.

The trails at Diamond A traverse gentle hills and grassy meadows. They pass through an apple orchard and across numerous creeks. You can even ride through the canopy created by the trees at either side of the old Danielson-to-Providence trolley track that runs through the property. If you like horses and the New England woodlands, come here.

For a unique family adventure, make reservations for Diamond A's **Wild West Trail Ride and Cookout.** Specially designed for families with young children, these trips are arranged by reservation only and usually consist of one- or two-family groups. Any day of the week, you leave the stables about an hour before dark and take a one-hour trail ride to a camp-site in the middle of the woods. There, a blazing campfire awaits you, com-plete with a steaming iron kettle of beans and a big old coffeepot for brew-ing river coffee. You eat beef jerky, beans, and biscuits or cornbread, and you sit around the campfire for an hour or two and tell tales and sing camp-fire songs until it's time to head back to the stables. Every cowpunch gets a bandana to take home. Little cowpokes might even get to wear a pair of six-shooters 'round the campfire. All this fun costs $25.00 per person six years old and older. Children up to six years old riding double with a par-ent pay just $6.00.

Other trips are available as well, including a three-and-a-half-hour trail ride to a pizza restaurant overlooking a lake. Warm yourselves with pizza by the stone fireplace in the restaurant and then head back to the sta-bles. The Pizza King Trail Rides (and meal) cost $35 for the first person, $30 for the second, and $25 for each person thereafter. Overnight camp-ing excursions leave from a trailhead in Natchaug State Forest and ride to the Lost Silvermine Horse Camp deep within the forest. All meals and sup-plies are included in the price of the trips; you just bring a sleeping bag and pillow. For rates and information, call 779–3000.

ONECO

You're not likely to find the village of Oneco by yourself unless you're afi-cionados of driving the blue highways. We love to take the road less trav-eled, but the demands of our schedule rarely allow serendipity to manifest itself. One day, however, we got lucky in Windham County. Not far from the interstate in the township of Sterling rests the sleepy intersection of Route 14A and Newport Road. There you will find a Connecticut master-piece—**Whitford's General Store** in Oneco village. Even if you have no other reason to come to Sterling township, bring the kids here for a peek at the merchandise in stock at this throwback to the good old days.

Proprietor Hedi Zicnowicz and her son Steve keep this place brimful of everything under the sun, and the inventory is carefully maintained with the guiding philosophy that if they don't have it, you don't need it. Stroll the aisles of the big old house that has contained this store since 1879;

they're lined with shelves of great old-time goods, some of which you might have thought no one manufactured anymore.

From almanacs to zippers, the merchandise will astound you. They have one-piece longjohns with a trap-door, night crawlers, fishing lures, blue jeans, barn boots, penny and nickel candy, cow manure—the list could take hours to recite. I know where you can buy pig and sow pellets, I just can't tell you whether you use them to feed 'em, cure 'em, or grow 'em. Hedi and Steve know, though, and they'll be pleased to tell you.

They'll also be happy to convince you to set a spell and have a plateful of their home cooking. They're not boasting when they claim to have gigantic grinders, fabulous fish and chips, huge hamburgers, outrageous onion rings, celebrated clam cakes, and a milkshake so thick you can stand your spoon up in it. Come in the morning for their Belly Buster, a grinder made with three eggs, sausage, bacon, ham, and cheese. You may have to carry the kids back to the car even if they share one of these. If, by some aberration of appetite or chemistry, the Buster doesn't satisfy, have a scoop or two of the Hershey's ice cream they serve out on the wide veranda in the summertime.

Whitford's is just a short way off exit 88 of I–395, so if you're passing through, pass through here first on your way to elsewhere. It's open year-round, Monday through Saturday from 6:00 A.M. to 10:00 P.M. and Sunday from 6:00 A.M. to 9:00 P.M. For information, call 564–5215.

POMFRET

Up near Pomfret you'll find **Mashomoquet Brook State Park.** Its nearly 1,000 acres are the combined area of three smaller parks: Wolf Den, Saptree Run, and Mashamoquet Brook. Some great trails link the areas and make this one of Connecticut's most popular state parks.

Several interesting features distinguish the park. At the entrance on Route 44, you'll find the **Brayton Grist Mill and Marcy Blacksmith Shop Museum,** both maintained by the Pomfret Historical Society. Billy Brayton's four-story gristmill is the state's finest example of a one-man water-powered mill operation of the 1890s. The equipment for generating power to grind grain and shell corn survives in the exact locations where Brayton used them. The turbine, the millstone, and a corn sheller are among the items you'll learn about on a tour of the museum.

On the mill's fourth level, an exhibit of handcrafted tools represents the labor of the Marcy family blacksmiths, who plied their trade from 1817 to 1946 in an area known as Marcy Hollow at the side of Mashamoquet Brook. Orin Marcy opened the shop in 1830, using a water-powered bellows and triphammer. A collection of tools made by the blacksmiths includes some used in the manufacture of wheels and horseshoes. In fact, Orin's son, Darius, earned first prize for his horseshoes at the Chicago World's Fair in 1893. There is no charge to tour the site. It is open on weekends from late May through September from 2:00 to 5:00 P.M.

In addition to hiking, fishing, and picnicking, Mashamoquet Brook State Park offers swimming and camping. Near the fifty-five open and wooded sites perfect for families are such amenities as flush toilets, drinking water, changing houses, picnic shelters, and a food concession.

The most famous of park features are the Table Rock and Indian Chair stone formations and the nearby **Putnam Wolf Den Trail.** General Israel Putnam became famous for more than just his role in the Revolutionary War and his famed ride against the British down the one hundred stone steps of his Greenwich hillside homestead. You see, he spent his young manhood in these parts, successfully pursuing dual careers of innkeeper and farmer.

Legend has it that for several years Israel and his neighbors were bothered by the killing instincts of a lone wolf that occasionally made a meal of the local livestock. One night in 1742 the wolf awakened the protective instincts of Israel by making off with more than just a few of Israel's sheep. Israel vowed to bring the killer down and assembled a ragtag army of neighbors to help him do it. For days Israel, his neighbors, and their hounds tracked the wolf, finally finding her lair in the face of a high cliff. In went the hounds braying and barking, and out they came again, yelping and mewling. None of them would reenter the cave.

Israel himself decided to go in after the beast. After a few almost comic attempts to apprehend the criminal, he was finally successful. He shot her and dragged her out by the ears. Some say she was the last wolf to live in Connecticut.

Today you can hike to her den via the park's Wolf Den Trail. Guided walks are offered from time to time; call for a schedule if you'd like to get the full story of Israel and the Wolf. You can also get the scoop by asking the rangers for a self-guided tour map. After you've seen the site of this sinister encounter, check out the natural formations of Indian Chair and Table Rock. They are just a little farther along the Wolf Den Trail.

The park is open year-round daily from 8:00 A.M. to sunset for day visitors. A $5.00 per car fee is charged only on weekends and holidays. Campers should make reservations for this popular site; the nightly rate for 1994 was $10.00 per campsite. You can also take your chances and arrive unannounced; vacancies are filled on a first come/first served basis. For information, call the Park Office at 928–6121.

THOMPSON

Some people think Thompson is the quintessential town of the Quiet Corner. Tiny and serene, it is lined with houses, churches, inns, and shops that seem eerily reminiscent of the eighteenth century. Were the town managers to outlaw automobile traffic, this village that grew alongside the stagecoach route to Boston and Providence would be surreal indeed.

A stroll along the main avenue of town is pleasant for parents and patient children, but the real family value in Thompson lies off the main thoroughfare in **Quaddick State Park.** Unless you've had your fill of simple pleasures, I think you'll find Quaddick a great place to spend an afternoon. Located on East Putnam Road off Route 44, the land and the lake were once the summer camp and fishing ground of the Nipmuck Indians. Later this place was the Thompson town farm, where the elderly citizens of the area spent their dotage in peaceful contemplation.

It's a fair bit noisier now, being actually one of the most popular state parks in the county. Its 466-acre reservoir and sandy beach are the source of most of the activity. You can swim, fish, sail, and canoe here in the summertime. Those delights are made easier with such facilities as changing houses, restrooms, a boat launch ramp, canoe rentals, a food concession, and drinking water. You can also hike through 166 acres of well-marked woodland trails or play ball on the sports field.

In winter you can ice-skate or ice-fish on the reservoir as long as the weather permits. Cross-country skiing is not possible on the trails, but you can hike or snowshoe if the spirit moves you to take the kids out for a brisk trek in the crisp air. Quaddick is open year-round from 8:00 A.M. to sunset. Admission is free, except on weekends and holidays in the summer when there is a $5.00 per car charge. For information, call 928–9200.

WILLIMANTIC/WINDHAM

Windham County has a little toe that pops westward from the lowest portion of its boundary with Tolland County. It is here that you'll find the small city of Willimantic and its sibling village of Windham. Situated on the banks of the Shetucket River, Willimantic's history is tied firmly to the textile mills that dominated three centuries of Connecticut industry.

In fact, many Windham County towns would have been altered were it not for the textile mills built along the Quinebaug and Shetucket rivers in the eighteenth and nineteenth centuries. Visit the **Windham Textile and History Museum** at 157 Union–Main Street, which is Route 66, to learn more about life in Connecticut's mill villages.

The first textile mill in Windham County was built in 1806 by Smith Wilkinson on the Quinebaug near present-day Putnam. It was a small cotton mill that depended on the fluctuating level of the river to drive its wheels and turbines. Soon the technology developed to control the water through the use of reservoirs, dams, and canals. It was only a matter of time before every town and village on the rivers had a textile mill. Thousands of immigrants poured into the region to work in the mills and make their homes in the towns. The Quinebaug Mill, built in Killingly in 1852, was one of the largest plants. It had 61,340 spindles, 1,656 looms, and produced 28 miles of cloth each day.

The Textile and History Museum examines the lives and culture of the people who labored in the mills. It also explores the stories of those who developed the technology and collected the money earned from the labor of immigrants at the height of the Industrial Revolution.

Located in two buildings of the former Willimantic Linen Company, the museum has an authenticity unsurpassed by any other re-creations in the region. Dugan Mill houses exhibits that bring the visitor right into the last century, when tens of thousands of workers labored under difficult conditions and for very low pay. The exhibits include re-creations of an 1880s mill shop floor, equipped with a carding machine, a spinning frame, a loom, and a textile printer. Above the shop is the overseer's office, from which the productivity of the workers was carefully monitored.

The museum's main building houses The Company Store, a re-creation of the shop that on this site once served the needs of the employees. It now doubles as the museum gift shop. A laborers' tenement, a mill agent's mansion from the Victorian era, and the 1877 Dunham Hall Library are also housed in the main building.

The museum is well worth a visit, especially if you plan to visit some of the region's mill sites. A handy driving tour brochure to the principal sites is available at the museum. The museum provides an excellent overview of the cultural and economic changes brought about by both the development and demise of the Connecticut textile industry. It is open Thursday through Sunday from noon to 5:00 P.M. Admission for adults is $3.00; children pay $1.00. For information, call 456–2178.

WOODSTOCK

Of all the Windham County towns, Woodstock may be the most gentrified and the most artsy. Comprised of villages named North Woodstock, South Woodstock, and so on, the town center most noted for its picturesque qualities is Woodstock proper, a sedate community located on beautiful Route 169. Atop the hill, its pretty town common beckons to the traveler with an eye for tranquil spaces.

If you allow the children to wander a while on the common, it shouldn't take them long to find **Roseland Cottage** just across the road. A candy-colored confection of a house, it is a most surprising attraction that provides at least an afternoon's worth of entertainment. Built in 1846 in the newly fashionable Gothic Revival style, this magnificent home was the summer retreat of Henry C. Bowen, native to Woodstock but long and successfully a New York dry goods dealer.

Though he made and lost several fortunes in his lifetime, Bowen never lost the sense of stewardship and philanthropy that characterized his actions. Founder of churches, abolitionist and supporter of the Union cause in the Civil War, advocate of the beautification of common property, Bowen was also, quite simply, a party animal. Mover and shaker in all kinds of social and political circles, Bowen liked nothing better than throwing a party for all to enjoy. Roseland Cottage was the site of many extravagant festivities—lawn parties, teas, bowling parties in the indoor bowling alley, and Fourth of July celebrations that made all others look dull in comparison.

A visit to this house on one of its special festival days is everything but dull, an appropriate tribute to its former owner. In addition to taking a tour of the fabulously luxurious "cottage," which retains most of its original furnishings, you can wander in the labyrinth of the formal parterre gardens, have a picnic under one of the many beautiful plantings on the lawn, and play games of the nineteenth century with other visitors.

The most popular family event is the Children's Lawn Party in early August. It features traditional games such as hoop rolling, ninepins, graces, and bilboquet. Children can also play marbles, jacks, or croquet. The staff serves lemonade and cookies; families are encouraged to bring picnics and eat on the lawn. A peanut hunt, storytelling, a musical parade your kids can join, and hat-decorating supplies for attiring yourselves in an appropriately festive manner are included in the $2.00 admission to this event.

An American Girls Party features Victorian revelry for any children seven and up, with or without an American Girls doll at their side. Discussions of the language of flowers and the history of teas, parasols, fans, and other Victoriana is part of the entertainment provided by the costumed hostess. You might also want to come for the Fall Festival of Arts and Crafts, which features tours, clowns, and jugglers to entertain the children, and a juried show of nearly 200 artisans. You might not be able to resist coming for tea with Mrs. Tiggy-Winkle, the delightfully incarnated hedgehog character from the tales of Beatrix Potter. Usually held in mid-July, this popular event is designed for children ages three to seven.

Many other events fill the calendar at Roseland Cottage. Call the number below for a complete schedule of the various garden parties, lawn concerts, and afternoon teas that are offered. The house, by the way, is incredible, and the gardens are breathtaking. No excess or expense seems to have been spared in their construction or decoration. You're going to be impressed, even if you have seen other homes as grand as this one.

Roseland Cottage is open Memorial Day through Labor Day, Wednesday through Sunday, with tours at noon, 1:00, 2:00, 3:00, and

4:00 P.M. After Labor Day weekend through mid-October, it is open Friday through Sunday, with tours at the same hours. Admission is $4.00 for adults; children twelve and under pay $2. For information, call 928–4074.

When you tire of the festival atmosphere of one of Mr. Bowen's parties, take a leisurely stroll or drive through Woodstock Center. It has many lovely places in which to browse, buy country treasures, or pick up something tasty to eat. Our favorites are the **Christmas Barn** and **Resourceful Judith,** both on Route 169. If you're hungry and nary a picnic basket is in sight, head to Route 198 via Route 171 and stop at **Stoggy Hollow General Store and Restaurant** for sandwiches of major proportions in all varieties and some pretty good salads for herbivores.

Casual, comfortable, and perfect for families, the two dining rooms of the restaurant are decorated with great old photographs of early twentieth-century Woodstock and the village of Stoggy Hollow. Read the back of your menu for the story of the origin of the name of the village. When you finish your lunch, be sure to stop by the bakery case on the market side of the restaurant. The pies and muffins are excellent.

From Stoggy Hollow, just head north to 1728 Route 198 for the last stop on your tour of Windham County. I couldn't say the **Photomobile Model Museum** is the best attraction in the area, but it is inarguably the most unusual. You are looking head on at the Future in this "world's first" museum of solar electric small-scale model vehicles.

About sixty models of cars, boats, trains, and planes are housed in the museum. A tour guide will teach you about solar-powered vehicles and their possible impact on transportation and the environment in the next century. Visitors over the age of about five can purchase and construct their own solar-powered models. Kits for miniature cars and boats can be opened and worked on with the help of a guide, or you can do your construction at home. Outside, on warm, sunny days, visitors can ride a solar-powered golf cart around the 33-acre property and paddle a full-sized solar-powered canoe.

Though completely unkempt, like the workshop of an absent-minded professor, the museum is thought-provoking and intriguing. You can look forward to some lively conversations as you drive away. Come on weekends year-round from 10:00 A.M. to 5:00 P.M. Saturday and noon to 5:00 P.M. Sunday. Admission is $2.00 for adults and $1.00 for children. For more information, call 974–3910.

NEW LONDON COUNTY

his county, on the southeastern shoreline of Connecticut, defies char-
acterization. First, the county comprises a wide variety of habitats.
The hills and forests of its northern region are distinctly different from
the meadows and marshes of its southern border along the Sound.
Secondly, the populations of the two areas are equally disparate. The peace-
able hills to the north are much like Windham County in the state's so-
called Quiet Corner, while the bustling towns of the shoreline reflect their
long history of industry and commerce.

Both areas provide an abundance of attractions and activities for families. From fine art gallery to lighthouse museum, from woodland trail to
fishing pier, with every level of sophistication and simplicity, New London's
sights are as diverse as the county's geography and demographics.

COLCHESTER

This town is typical of the northern communities of New London County.
Elegant houses surround its green; small shops, a few restaurants, and pretty public buildings provide the hub of a structure that is primarily rural in
nature. Don't let it fool you that Colchester calls its main drag "Broadway."
This really is a country town.

That's a fact easy to accept when you're out on Route 149 at **Day
Pond State Park.** Originally constructed by a pioneering family named

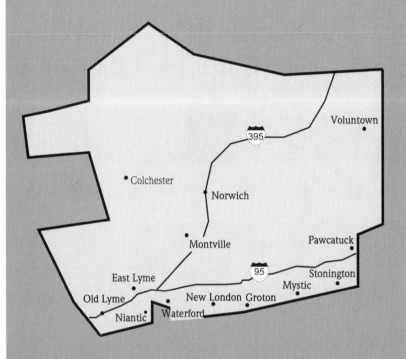

Voluntown

• Colchester

• Norwich

Montville

Pawcatuck

95

East Lyme

Stonington

Old Lyme

New London Groton

Mystic

Niantic Waterford

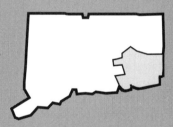

New London County

Day, the pond is an antique mill pond, the water of which once turned an overshot waterwheel that powered the up-and-down saw of the family's sawmill. Now empty of all signs of industry, the pond is stocked regularly with trout and is popular with fishers, swimmers, and skaters.

A 4-mile loop trail is an easy walk for families; it connects with a 2½-mile trail to the Comstock Bridge on the Salmon River. The combination of the two trails makes for a great day hike. Pack a lunch and eat at the 1873 covered bridge. Bring along a few night crawlers and a couple of poles and hooks, and you'll have the makings of a perfect country day.

As is typical, the state has provided telephones, toilets, picnic tables, and drinking water. Admission is free, except on weekends and holidays when you pay a $5.00 parking fee. The park is open daily year-round from 8:00 A.M to sunset. For information, call 295–9523.

If you have no desire to prepare a lunch, stop first at **Harry's Place** on Route 16 back near the center of town. It's about as classic a roadside stand as ever stood on an American highway. Open only from April 15 to October 1, Harry's Place was recently called "the ultimate burger joint" by the *Hartford Courant.* No waistline-trimming foods are served here—just burgers dripping with "juice," excellent onion rings, french fries, hot dogs, and sauerkraut. Wash these down with soft drinks and shakes while you sit at the picnic tables set up right near the road. Harry's Place has been "proud to serve" since 1918, so maybe there's a secret to longevity in this greasy gastronomy. Check it out.

Colchester is a great place for parents looking for game and craft bargains. Stop at the **World Wide Games** factory outlet on Mill Street for the chance to pay up to 90 percent off retail for discontinued, slightly irregular, or damaged classic wooden board games, puzzles, and brainteasers. You can also buy arts and crafts supplies, kits for recreational therapy and Bible study, and much more. They are open Tuesday, Wednesday, and Friday from 9:00 A.M. to 4:30 P.M.; Thursday from 9:00 A.M. to 6:00 P.M.; and Saturday from 10:00 A.M. to 4:00 P.M. For information, call 537–2325.

GROTON

Not too long ago, it could have been a toss-up as to which town— Colchester or Groton—would be the quieter of the two. Bustling Groton was in danger of having a mostly unemployed workforce and a ghost-town downtown when the United States Naval Reserve Station almost pulled up stakes and left town.

Back on an even keel since the Navy decided to stay, Groton remains a busy center of naval and defense-related industry. Its long history as such defines its attractions as well. Surrounded on three sides by the waters of Long Island Sound, the Thames River, and the Mystic River, Groton has been a leading shipbuilding center since the eighteenth century. For much of the last century, it has been most famed as the home of the Electric Boat Division of General Dynamics, the leading designer and manufacturer of nuclear submarines.

Visitors to the area will see the U.S. Naval Submarine Base and the Naval Submarine School and can visit the **USS *Nautilus,*** the world's first nuclear submarine. The **USS *Nautilus* Memorial** at the U.S. Naval Submarine Base on Route 12 includes tours of the *Nautilus* and an award-winning museum that explores the history and technology of submarines.

Excellently presented in a state-of-the-art facility, the exhibits celebrate the achievements of the human mind in devising this technology. Children can stand in the re-created sub attack center and hear the sounds of battle. They can operate three working periscopes. They can watch films of submarine history, and they can explore four mini-subs outside and a variety of models inside. Other outstanding exhibits explain the important uses of the submarine in both defense and underwater exploration.

Aboard the *Nautilus* you will explore the sonar and torpedo rooms and the navigation and control room. You will visit the crew's living quarters, the galley, the captain's quarters, and much more. Visitors will easily imagine life and work aboard this amazing vessel that explored beneath Arctic ice and the 20,000 leagues of the deep.

Open year-round April 15 to October 14, 9:00 A.M. to 5:00 P.M. daily, except Tuesday, when it opens at 1:00 P.M., and October 15 to April 14, from Wednesday through Monday from 9:00 A.M. to 4:00 P.M. The museum is also closed the first full week of May and the first full two weeks of December, plus Thanksgiving, Christmas, and New Year's Day. Admission and parking are free. For information, call (800) 343–0079 or 449–3174.

The lure of the sea may capture you here. If so, head to the Institute of Marine Science at the Avery Point campus of the University of Connnecticut (Benham Road). There you can board *Enviro-Lab* for a two-and-a-half-hour cruise called **Project Oceanology.** These summer expeditions are among the best family activities offered in the state, especially for those families with a child interested in the study of marine biology.

Enviro-Lab's instructors are marine scientists and teachers who accompany each group of about 25 passengers for an afternoon or morning of study. Using the same methods the scientists use in their work, you will measure and record data about the geology and biology you observe. You will learn the uses of nautical charts and navigation instruments. You will collect and test water, mud, and sand samples. You will pull trawl nets and examine the plants and animals you catch. All the while you will be enjoying the beauty of the islands, lighthouses, and watercraft that surround your area of exploration.

Project Oceanology is operated by a nonprofit organization that teaches more than 20,000 schoolchildren during the school year. Public cruises are offered mid-June to Labor Day at 10:00 A.M. and 1:00 P.M. Adults pay $15.00; children under twelve pay $10.00. Reservations are strongly recommended; many cruises fill up before sailing time.

You should wear sunscreen or a hat and sneakers. Bring a sweatshirt or windbreaker. Soft drinks are available for purchase at the Project Oceanology building, but there is no food concession and you should not go aboard hungry. For information and reservations, call (800) 364–8472 between 9:00 A.M and 4:00 P.M.

If something nautical but a little less hands-on is what you have in mind, take the *River Queen* cruise at 193 Thames Street. This excursion boat cruises up the Thames past the *Nautilus,* the sub base, and the Coast Guard Academy on the New London side of the river. The schedules and fares vary, so for updated information, call 445–9516.

Revolutionary War buffs might want to visit **Fort Griswold Battlefield State Park** at Monument Street and Park Avenue. Site of the 1781 massacre of American defenders by British troops under the command of Benedict Arnold, the fort includes a 134-foot monument and a museum that tells the story of the battle. Also on the park grounds is the 1750 **Ebenezer Avery House,** which, in its original site on Thames

Street, had been a repository for some of the wounded patriots. Moved to the park in 1971, its kitchen and weaving room are furnished as they might have been in the eighteenth century.

The battlefield and fort ruins are open daily year-round from 9:00 A.M. to 5:00 P.M. The museum and monument are open Memorial Day to Labor Day from 9:00 A.M. to 5:00 P.M. and from the weekend after Labor Day until Columbus Day weekends only at the same hours. The Avery House is open only weekends from Memorial Day to Labor Day from 1:00 to 5:00 P.M. Admission is free to all sites at all times. For information, call 566–2304.

MONTVILLE

North of New London near the Thames River is the **Tantaquidgeon Indian Museum** at 1819 Norwich–New London Turnpike, which is Route 32. Filled with stone, bone, and wooden objects used or made mostly by the Mohegan Indians, this museum was founded by John Tantaquidgeon, a direct descendant of Uncas, chief of the Mohegans. The emphasis here is on the Mohegans and other Eastern Woodland tribes, but the collection also includes artifacts from Native people of the Southwest and the Northern Plains. Pottery, rugs, dolls, tools, and beaded bags, shoes, and other objects are among the items in this collection.

The culture and history of each group are explained throughout the exhibits. Open May through October Tuesday through Sunday from 10:00 A.M. to 4:00 p.m., the museum asks only for a donation from visitors. For information, call 848–9145.

The Montville area is rich in the history of the Mohegans. If you drive north on Route 32 to Raymond Hill Road, you will find Mohegan Hill and **Cochegan Rock,** which is supposedly the site of secret meetings between Uncas and other Mohegan leaders. Continue on Route 32 to the village of Mohegan, where in **Fort Shantok State Park** you will find the remains of a Mohegan village, the fort of Chief Uncas, and a Mohegan burial ground. The grave of Uncas himself is 4 miles north in Norwich on Sachem Street in the **Royal Indian Burial Ground.**

MYSTIC

If I were to name the ten towns in Connecticut that most typify the essence of New England, I surely would mention Mystic. Rich in history that harks back to the earliest days of the Connecticut Colony, it is a town that has witnessed the first of the difficult compromises between settler and native, the glory days of whaling and shipbuilding, the rise of industrialization, and the decline of agriculture. Throughout this history Mystic has remained a vital community comprised of diverse citizens engaged in the simple craft of building an American tradition.

For many years in this century, Mystic has been a tourist destination, most notably because of Mystic Seaport Museum, among the nation's most outstanding maritime history museums. Now home to other notable attractions, Mystic is a destination for more tourists than ever before in its history. Even its wonderful downtown, until somewhat recently unknown to out-of-towners, is now a thriving center enjoyed by tourists as well as townies.

The first stop in Mystic for most visitors is still the **Mystic Seaport Museum** on Route 27 off I–95 exit 90. Its seventeen acres of historic buildings and re-creations represent a nineteenth-century New England whaling and shipbuilding village. An incredible array of educational and entertainment activities are offered here throughout the year. From ropemaking to printing to oystering, from sailor to chandler to merchant, the arts, crafts, and occupations of an early American seaport are celebrated with and demonstrated for visitors of all ages.

Horse and buggy rides, planetarium shows, sea chantey sing-alongs, chowder festivals, lantern-light holiday dramas, tall ship tours, summer camps, living-history workshops, boat excursions, concerts, and more are among the opportunities for family adventure.

If you haven't already visited here, you must plan to do so soon. You may find yourself riding a turn-of-the-century bicycle, stitching a sailor's log book, or sampling a hearty New England stew. I can't recall a time when a visit here hasn't prompted one of our girls to say, "Oh, I wish we could live here!" You'll love it, too, I predict.

Mystic Seaport Museum is open year-round daily, except Christmas Day. In summer, the schedule is 9:00 A.M. to 8:00 P.M.; from October to April, it opens at 10:00 A.M. and closes at 4:00 P.M. Spring and early autumn hours fall somewhere between the two. Adult admission is $15.00; children six through fifteen pay $7.50; five and younger are free. Family memberships are usually good bargains if you have more than two

The seal pools are just one exciting stop at the Mystic Marinelife Aquarium. (Courtesy Connecticut's Mystic and More/Mystic Marinelife Aquarium)

kids and you're coming twice in a year. For information, call 572–5315.

Mystic Marinelife Aquarium (55 Coogan Boulevard, off I–95, exit 90) is the area's second largest attraction. Built about twenty years ago with a mission of education, research, and conservation, Mystic Marinelife Aquarium also has much to offer in the way of entertainment. Its primary focus is the education, and in this effort it does an outstanding job.

More than 6,000 marine mammals are displayed in fifty exhibits from New England tidal marsh to tropical reef and penguin paradise. Indoor and outdoor exhibits include large marine mammals such as beluga whales and dolphins, several species of sharks, seals, and sea lions, hundreds of species of fish, and invertebrates of every sort. The Seal Island and Penguin Pavilion exhibits are exceptional re-creations of the animals' natural habitats. The marine theater allows staff marine biologists to demonstrate the talents and capabilities of dolphins, seals, and belugas.

Mystic Marinelife Aquarium also hosts workshops, classes, and special events throughout the year. Explore the undersea world any day except New Year's Day, the last full week in January, Thanksgiving, and Christmas. It opens at 9:00 A.M. and close at 4:30 P.M. Summer hours extend to 5:30 P.M. Adult admission is $9.00; children five through twelve pay $5.50; under-fives are free. For information, call 536–3323.

Immediately adjacent to Mystic Marinelife Aquarium is **Olde Mistick Village** at the junction of Route 27 and Coogan Boulevard. A shopping center built as a re-creation of a circa-1720 New England village, its pretty paths, reproduction shops, ponds, fences, and waterwheels make for very pleasant shopping. Franklin's General Store, Elizabeth and Harriet's Fine Handcrafts, and Wind and Wood are our favorite shops. Restaurants, jewelry stores, clothing and toy shops, gourmet coffee and chocolate shops, and much more are here.

Olde Mistick Village is especially attractive in summer when its ponds are busy with waterfowl, its gazebo is the site of free concerts, and its flowers are in bloom. During December the village is aglow with holiday displays and various festivities and promotions in individual shops. Open year-round daily, Monday through Saturday from 10:00 A.M. to 6:00 P.M. and Sunday from noon to 5:00 P.M. For information, call 536–4941.

If you need a break from the marine and historical themes, visit the **Denison Pequotsepos Nature Center** on Pequotsepos Road (follow Coogan Boulevard to its eastern end, take a right onto Jerry Browne Road, then right onto Pequotsepos). This 125-acre preserve has 7 miles of trails through woods and meadows. Wildflower and fern gardens are among the areas developed to encourage homeowners to create their own similar backyard habitats. A nice feature here is the so-called Peace Sanctuary atop a hill overlooking the Mystic River.

A natural-history museum includes indoor native wildlife exhibits and outdoor flight enclosures for nonreleasable raptors. The Trading Post gift shop sells field guides, children's books, birding supplies, and natural science materials for children. A full schedule of guided walks, summer camps, and field trips can be obtained at the museum.

The center is open November 1 to April 30, Tuesday through Saturday from 9:00 A.M. to 4:00 P.M. and Sunday from noon to 4:00 P.M.; May 1 through October 31, it is open Tuesday through Saturday from 9:00 A.M. to 5:00 P.M. and Sunday from noon to 5:00 P.M. Adult admission is $3.00; children pay $1.00; under-fives are free. Call 536–1216.

If your appetite for the sea has been whetted, head to Route 1 via

Route 27 and the famed counterweighted bascule drawbridge that leads you to picturesque historic downtown Mystic. Linger on the bridge itself (park the car somewhere else first) and watch the boats, jellyfish, and other flotsam. Stroll the shops, art galleries, and bookstores. This is a wonderful village. Discover your own favorites, but be sure to stop by the incredible Mystic's Army Navy Store, Mystical Toys, the Mystic Drawbridge Ice Cream Company, and the incomparable Sea Swirl seafood shack.

NEW LONDON

Like its sister city, Groton, across the Thames River, New London has a long maritime history that has influenced its development into a center of commerce and industry. Settled in 1646 as Pequot Plantation by John Winthrop, Jr., it was by 1846 the second largest whaling port in the world. Long a manufacturing and shipbuilding city, New London offers an eclectic assortment of attractions of value to families.

If someone in your family has an interest in the Coast Guard, you should know that New London is the home of the **United States Coast Guard Academy** on Mohegan Avenue off Route 31, overlooking the river. It offers a free visitors center and museum, plus tours of the barque USCG *Eagle* whenever it is in port. Dress parades and concerts by the Coast Guard Band are offered on a seasonal schedule. Call 444–8270.

New London is also the home of the **Lyman Allyn Museum,** near the Academy at 625 Williams Street. Like the New Britain Museum of American Art, the Lyman Allyn owns one of Connecticut's little-known but exceptional art collections. Fine and decorative arts from America, Europe, Asia, and the South Pacific make this a perfect introduction to art history for children. This beautiful neo-classical museum contains some holdings of special appeal to children. An Egyptian falcon mummy, Victorian dolls, toys, and dollhouses, and Native American artifacts are among these.

The museum arranges changing exhibitions with children in mind twice yearly, usually in the summer and between Thanksgiving and New Year's Day. One recent exhibition celebrated the work of New England children's book illustrators; another featured dollhouses and miniatures. Art classes for children are offered from time to time throughout the year.

The museum is open year-round, with the exception of Mondays and major holidays. From June 1 to Labor Day the hours are Tuesday through Saturday from 10:00 A.M. to 5:00 P.M., Sunday from 1:00 to 5:00 P.M., and late closing Wednesday, at 9:00 P.M. After Labor Day until May 31, they are open Tuesday through Friday and Sunday from 1:00 to 5:00 P.M., Saturday from 11:00 A.M. to 5:00 P.M., and Wednesday until 9:00 P.M. Adult admission is $3.00; students pay $2.00, and children twelve and under are free. For information, call 443–2545.

While you are still in an educational frame of mind, visit the historic **Hempsted Houses** at 11 Hempstead Street in the historic downtown area. One of these two structures is among the oldest documented houses in America; both are among the few New London structures to have survived the burning of the city in 1781 by the British troops under the command of Benedict Arnold.

Ten generations of the Hempsted family lived on this soil, and the diaries of Joshua Hempsted have contributed greatly both to the excellent interpretation of the house itself and to our knowledge of eighteenth-century colonial American life. The 1678 Joshua Hempsted House is one of the oldest frame buildings in New England. The newer 1759 Nathaniel Hempsted House is one of the most unusual historic homes in New England—it has 2-foot-thick stone walls, a gambrel roof, and an exterior projecting beehive oven.

The houses are open from mid-May to Columbus Day, Thursday through Sunday from noon to 5:00 P.M. Activities for children are offered on one weekend each month. On Labor Day weekend a special focus is given to women's work of the eighteenth century. A Hempsted Thanksgiving is celebrated the Saturday after the holiday. Costumed docents, open-hearth cooking, and food samples add to the vivid pre–Revolutionary War ambience of the festivities. An excellent colonial life summer camp is offered for children ages eight to twelve or so. Admission is $4.00 for adults and $1.00 for children. For information, call 443–7949.

For the kind of family fun wherein everybody gets wet, come to **Ocean Beach Park,** which offers not one, but three ways to get soaked. Right on the Sound at 1225 Ocean Avenue, Ocean Beach Park is both old-fashioned public beach resort and newfangled conference facility.

A half-mile long, very clean, white sand beach is the focal point of the

park. A full staff of lifeguards and a first-aid station help make this a popular destination for families. Volleyball nets, outdoor children's movies, and
teen dances are provided to keep families busy all day. An immaculate
Olympic-sized swimming pool and a beautiful brand-new bathhouse with
changing rooms, lockers, and showers are also available for individual fees.

Ocean Beach Park also has a wonderful wide wooden boardwalk
down the length of the beach. It leads past food concessions, a game
arcade, and a miniature golf course complete with life-sized spouting
sperm whale.

Once the site of carnival-style kiddie rides, the park now has just one
remaining amusement park–style waterslide. A humdinger of a ride, it is,
with the exception of the beach itself, the most popular attraction here.
Operated by a separate concession, it is a triple-run, three-speed tower of
serpentine slides. A height requirement of 46 inches helps keep the ride
safe for all visitors. Young children cannot ride double with a parent or sibling, and the folks in charge are strict about the guidelines, so don't expect
to be able to smuggle anyone through on tiptoes.

The flumes begin about 50 feet up at the top of a challenging set of
stairs. Depending on your speed and stamina in climbing those stairs while
carrying a rubbery mat, you'll get ten to fifteen runs down the flume of
your choice in a half-hour time slot. Each person pays $4.50 for a half-hour,
or each of you can have unlimited rides throughout a whole day for
$10.00. Our kids like the medium flume best; the fast one is fun, but small
kids are tossed around a bit at the bottom; we came home with a few
elbows rubbed raw. By the way, the view from the tower is fabulous.

Ocean Beach is open Memorial Day weekend through Labor Day
weekend from 8:00 A.M. to midnight. Admission is collected through a
parking fee of 75 cents per half-hour with an $8.50 maximum per car. Use
of the slide, pool, lockers, and mini-golf involves extra per-person or per-
family charges. For information, call 447–3301 or (800) 962–0284.

A variety of sailing opportunities leave from New London's docks.
Check among these for trips that fit your family's interests and budget:

The **Block Island Ferry** leaves from Ferry Street once each day from
mid-June to mid-September for a round trip to Old Harbor, Block Island.
The *Anna C* leaves New London at 9:00 A.M. and arrives at Old Harbor at

11:00 A.M. It leaves Old Harbor at 4:30 P.M., docking in New London at 6:30 P.M. Cars, walkers, and bicycles are welcome. Block Island is a wonderful family cycling destination. Call 442–7891.

Out O' Mystic Schooner Cruises offers three-day pirate adventures in search of buried treasure on a secret island, plus half-day luncheon cruises, dinner cruises, and one- to five-day sneak-away cruises along the New England coast. The *Mystic Clipper* and the *Mystic Whaler* leave from Shaw's Cove at 56 Howard Street, May through October. Call 437–0385.

Voyager Cruises uses the *Argia,* a reproduction nineteenth-century gaff-rigged schooner, and the *Voyager,* a traditional windjammer schooner, to make half-day, full-day, and getaway cruises to Fisher's Island and Sag Harbor, New York, as well as to Block Island. Summer departures sail from Steamboat Wharf. Call 536–0416.

NIANTIC/EAST LYME

Another of the shore villages, Niantic is hardly more than a hamlet—you'll drive through it before you even realize you were there. Actually a section of the town of East Lyme, Niantic is a village of private homes and beaches, marinas, and fishing piers.

Near the handful of specialty shops on its Main Street (Route 156 off Route 161 off exit 74 of I–95) is the **Children's Museum of Southeastern Connecticut.** This small facility is excellent for young children, and it is perhaps the most up-and-coming of Connecticut's similar interactive museums designed especially for children ages one to eight.

More a play area and experience center than a traditional museum, the Children's Museum features an area called Kidville, where young children can role-play in its health center, radio station, schoolhouse, fire station, grocery store, and lobster boat. The natural sciences, the arts, safety and health, and culture and history are explored through activities and exhibits in the arts and crafts center, the CD-ROM learning center, the Science Discovery Room, and the outdoor animal habitat and picnic areas.

The museum also offers changing exhibitions. A recent example was *Moonwalk—25 Years Later,* which featured items from the U.S. space exploration program on loan from NASA. In the process of development, the museum has been awarded a grant from the Connecticut Humanities Council to create a traveling exhibition on cultural diversity. An interactive HO-scale model of the historic passenger service between New Haven and Mystic will share space in the changing exhibition room with that future exhibit.

A great rainy-day place if you are vacationing in the area, the museum is open year-round, Tuesday through Sunday and any Monday that school is not in session. The hours are 9:00 A.M. to 4:00 P.M. Tuesday through Saturday and open Mondays, noon to 4:00 P.M. Sunday. Admission is $3.00 for each person age two and up.Call 691–1255.

Speaking of vacations, few better places exist for shore camping and hiking than **Rocky Neck State Park** in Niantic/East Lyme. Its full mile of beach frontage on Long Island Sound provides swimming, beachcombing, fishing, and scuba diving opportunities; its 150-plus campsites provide a home away from home for professional beach bums, amateur naturalists, and the children thereof.

Interpretive programs, junior naturalist activities, and a full summer calendar of lectures, walks, and slide shows are offered for campers as well as day visitors. Campers have drinking water and bathrooms with showers and toilets. The state provides picnic shelters, bathhouses, food concessions, lifeguards, and telephones.

Rocky Neck is safe, clean, and open year-round. Charges for day use and camping vary. Summer visitors pay a daily fee, while off-season visitors pay a weekends-only fee or no fee at all. The campground is open April through October. With windswept bluffs and gorgeous views of the Sound and offshore islands, the park is one of the prettiest public shoreline areas. Open dawn to dusk in winter, the trails and open spaces can be used for cross-country skiing. For information, call 739–5471.

NORWICH

A small city with the unfortunate distinction of being the birthplace of Benedict Arnold, Norwich has maintained a fairly low profile as far as tourism is concerned. Nevertheless, this hilly city has a growing number of attractions that visiting families can enjoy.

First among them is the **Slater Memorial Museum** on the campus of the Norwich Free Academy at 108 Crescent Street. Founded in 1888, this museum is the place to take the children if you think it may be a while before you all can travel to the Louvre, the Vatican, the Olympia, or any other of the world's finest sculpture galleries.

Slater Memorial has a notable and beautiful collection of 150 plaster cast statues of famed sculptures from around the world. Among these exact reproductions of Greek, Roman, and Renaissance masterpieces are *Aphrodite* (the so-called "Venus de Milo") and Michelangelo's *Pietà.* I can't overstate the beauty of these pieces; truly, if you are at all interested in having your children see the unbelievable genius of Michelangelo, Donatello, Verrocchio, Luca della Robbia, and others, save yourself the airfare and come here.

The museum also houses a wonderful collection of American art from the seventeenth to twentieth centuries, plus American Indian artifacts and Oriental, African, and European art and textiles. The Gualtieri Gallery is especially appealing to children. Among other pieces, it contains dollhouses, dolls, and circus figures and furniture. The American Rooms are period rooms that trace American history from colonial to Victorian days. Ask the children at the outset of your visit to look for their favorite piece in the museum. The suggestion encourages them to look carefully, and they'll hardly notice the educational value of the treasure hunt.

The museum is open daily year-round, with the exception of holidays. From September through June, it is open Monday through Friday from 9:00 A.M. to 4:00 P.M. and Saturday and Sunday from noon to 4:00 P.M. In July and August, it is open Tuesday through Sunday from 1:00 to 4:00 P.M. Admission is free. For information, call 887–2506.

After a visit here, stop at **Mohegan Park** on Mohegan Park Road. Recently improved with walkways, plantings, statuary, and a fountain, the 385-acre woodland park is a lovely spot to spend an afternoon. Walking trails, picnic areas with grills and tables, and various pavilions and gazebos help make the park a family destination. The small **Mohegan Park Zoo** has monkeys, coyotes, and other small mammals, plus American eagles and domestic barnyard animals for feeding and petting. Near the park's pond is a swimming area perfect for young children; a play area with swings and such is also here. The award-winning roses in the park's formal gardens at Judd and Rockwell streets are in bloom from late May through October, peaking in late June and July.

Newly restored in Norwich and still a project under development is the **Upper Falls Heritage Park and Museum** on the banks of the Yantic River off Sherman Street. So brand-new that we haven't visited it ourselves, it is part of an ongoing attempt to preserve and restore the river and the various dams and mill buildings that contributed to Norwich's nineteenth- and twentieth-century history as a mill town.

The efforts to beautify and preserve the area include restoration of the dam, and thus the falls, the 1910 powerhouse (where the museum exhibits are housed and original machinery is on display), and the sacred site known as Indian Leap, where a group of Mohegans jumped to their deaths to escape the Narragansetts in 1643.

The 2-mile **Heritage Park Walkway** will link the Upper Falls Park and Museum with Indian Leap, the Lower Falls, and Norwich Harbor. This cycling/walking path is part of the National Heritage Corridor, a protected green belt along the Quinebaug and Shetucket rivers and their tributaries. The waterfront area of Norwich is also under redevelopment as a tourist area. An annual Harbor Day celebration in mid-August has helped to launch the revitalization of this historic area.

The Upper Falls Heritage Park and Museum were opened in fall 1994; hours for the current season can be obtained by calling 886–9846.

You should also know that in the nearby village of Taftville, just north of Mohegan Park on Route 169, is the **Quinnehticut Woolen Company Yarn Mill,** manufacturer of woolen yarn for knitting and weaving. Located in the Ponemah Mill complex built in 1871 as a water-powered cotton mill, the factory is open for tours. You can see the five steps necessary to turn raw sheep fleece into fine finished yarn, on machines that have changed little since the nineteenth century.

At one time reputed to be the largest cotton mill under one roof in the world, the Ponemah complex includes the mill, the mill workers' houses, and the company store (now the site of the woolen mill store). We have not yet taken this tour, so drop me a postcard to let me know if you liked it. Tours are given May 31 through December 31, Thursday through Saturday from 10:00 A.M. to 4:00 P.M. For information, call 889–0325.

OLD LYME

A curious mix of authors, painters, and mariners inhabit Old Lyme, a lovely village that revels in its artsy reputation as well as its nautical one. It's no surprise that Old Lyme can employ the phrase "colony" to describe itself— it has long attracted residents who fall neatly into one or more of these three categories.

One of the earliest and most permanent of these groups were the artists who gathered at the home of Florence Griswold from 1899 past the turn of the century. Known as the Lyme Art Colony, the folks who lived at Miss Florence's beautiful late-Georgian mansion played with light, color, and texture until they successfully settled upon characteristics later to become known as American Impressionism. J. Alden Weir, Childe Hassam, William Chadwick, and many others perfected their brilliance here. Now the lovely **Florence Griswold Museum** at 96 Lyme Street, the mansion holds a magnificent collection of these works and holds festivals and changing exhibitions to celebrate other artistry.

A Midsummer Festival includes all kinds of activities for children from typical pastimes like face painting and pony rides to unusual fun like knot-tying and scavenger hunts. Storytelling by the National Theater of the Deaf and Victorian children's games accompany an art show, silent auction, lawn concert, and more for the whole family.

Every December the mansion is decorated with Christmas trees in every room for the Christmas Tree Festival. Story readings and special tours of interest to children are offered during this time. We have been to this celebration, and it is lovely and very low-key. No visits from Santa or sticky candy canes—just beautiful trees and art.

The museum is open June through October, Tuesday through Saturday from 10:00 A.M. to 5:00 P.M. and Sunday from 1:00 to 5:00 P.M. From November through May, it is open Wednesday through Sunday, from 1:00 to 5:00 P.M. Adult admission is $3.00; children under twelve are free.

PAWCATUCK

The easternmost village just before you cross the Rhode Island border on I–95, Pawcatuck is just a speck of a place with a truly fun—*just for fun*— attraction called **Maple Breeze Park,** right off exit 92 on Liberty Street, which is Route 2. I promise you, there is nothing—*nothing*—educational about Maple Breeze Park. There is no history or legend associated with this

place. There is no scientific principle to understand, no mathematical concept to learn. There are absolutely no docents, costumed or otherwise. Just
bring a bathing suit and prepare to have a great time.

You can slide down either of two 350-foot-long waterslides. Wide,
smooth, and immaculate, these are tons of fun for anyone taller than roughly 40 inches. All riders must slide separately. You can also ride motorized
bumper boats; children have to be 48 inches tall to ride the boats alone, but
youngsters smaller than that can ride with taller siblings or parents. This is
wacky play—absolutely all decorum is thrown to the winds as you strive to
knock your family right out of its seat with your rampaging vessel of revenge.

You can also play eighteen holes of miniature golf here. Again, this is
immaculate and meticulously landscaped. Folks playing grown-up golf on
the country club course don't get greens as well groomed as these. Next to
the mini-golf are motorized kiddie karts. Cute as buttons for toddlers to
about eight-year-olds, these go round and round a track with not a whole
lot of purpose but a whole bunch of fun for little tykes.

Across the street are go-karts you reach through a tunnel that goes
under the road (and through which you can run screaming at the top of
your lungs just in case you're not already having enough fun). Your token
buys you four laps around a quarter-mile track. Small children can ride
with anyone over sixteen. This is great fun—we had a blast. Actually, this
may have some educational value . . . Never mind. Just have fun.

Use of all the rides and games is administered through the purchase
of tokens. Bumper boats cost $3.00 per person for a four-minute ride; the
go-karts also cost $3.00, but for a three-minute ride. Mini-golf is $4.00 per
person; the waterslide is $6.00 for a forty-minute turn.

Maple Breeze is open during May and June on weekends only from
10:00 A.M. to 10:00 P.M. and daily July 1 through Labor Day at the same
hours. A snack bar and the Main Family ice-cream stand (scrumptious ice
cream) are on the premises. For information, call 599–1232.

STONINGTON

This is my favorite Connecticut town. Someday I would like to live here in
a tiny house overlooking the sea, with lupines below my balcony and
kitchen herbs in my dooryard. One of my daughters loves this place, too,

so much so that she doesn't want me to tell you about it. "I don't want anyone else to go there," she says.

It is very quaint, very New England, very evocative of the days of sea captains and West Indies trading ships. Close your eyes and see the little girls playing hoops and graces, the little boys in knee-pants shinning their way up the flagpoles. Hear the clip-clopping of the horses, the whoosh of the gas lamps, the clanging of the bell buoys. It's all easy to imagine in Stonington.

Park anywhere here and just stroll. It's not that small, actually, but it's a great walking town. Go down Water Street to DuBois Beach right on the Point and soak up the salt air and sea breeze. Life doesn't get any better than this. Make your way through the shops and galleries, stop for a bite to eat at any of several great restaurants or casual cafes. Enjoy the model railroad in the Anguilla Gallery and the folk art at Buttercups.

Lastly, visit the **Old Lighthouse Museum** at 7 Water Street. Inside the 1832 stone lighthouse are displays of whaling and fishing equipment, swords and cannonballs and other instruments of defense, nineteenth-century portraits, and much more. One exhibit focuses on the wonderful treasures brought back to Stonington by the captains of the China trade route. Another shows a collection of antique shoes found in the walls of old houses to protect them from evil spirits. The antique dollhouse, decoys, toys, and model ships are especially interesting to children.

You can learn about the history of Stonington and its role in the War of 1812. You can learn about the railroad that once transferred passengers from sailing ships to river steamboats. You can even climb the tower of the lighthouse itself for a marvelous view of the harbor and the fishing fleet that still works in these waters.

The Museum is open daily in July and August from 11:00 A.M. to 5:00 P.M. In May, June, September, and October, it is open Tuesday through Sunday at the same hours. Admission is $2.00 for adults and $1.00 for children six through twelve. For information, call 535–1440.

WATERFORD

Waterford has a mall, movie theaters, and an amazing complex called Sonalysts Studios that may someday take Hollywood right off the map. Unfortunately, the mall and movies won't add much to a family vacation and neither will Sonalysts since they don't yet offer tours. Waterford nonetheless offers two attractions you might want to check out.

Down at the docks on First Street at Captain John's Sport Fishing Center, you can catch the captain's **Sunbeam Express Whale Watch Cruise** every Sunday (and perhaps in the future on some weekdays) from mid-June through Labor Day at 9:00 A.M. A naturalist is aboard for each trip, providing a fascinating narration on the animals, the ecology, and the environment. You can also watch the naturalist gathering data for cetacean research, such as the photographing and cataloging of distinctive marks to identify and track individual whales.

With the excellent navigation of Captain John or his son Captain Bob, you cruise the 22 miles to Montauk Point on Long Island and then search the waters in a 10- to 20-mile radius of Montauk and Block Island for fin whales, humpbacks, and the occasional sei or right whale. Captain John is himself very knowledgeable and committed to the protection of these whales. In radio communication with local fisherfolk, he has an 85 to 90 percent success rate of finding whales on these trips, but he can't guarantee that these magnificent wild creatures will cooperate with your plans to see them. The boat returns to Waterford between 2:00 and 3:00 P.M.

From mid-March to mid-May, Captain John goes out on seal watching trips; harbor and harp seals have returned to these waters in increasing numbers recently. From January through early March, the cruises leave from the Dock 'N Dine Restaurant in Old Saybrook and head up the Connecticut River for a look at the bald eagles that come from Canada to feed on white perch they grab from the sections of the river that remain unfrozen south of Haddam. Seal and eagle cruises depart at 9:00 A.M. and return around noon. All are naturalist-guided, and all are great for families. Each cruise highlights any wildlife you might see, from ospreys, herons, and other waterfowl to wild turkeys, fox, and deer on the riverbanks.

The crew bring lunches, snacks, and soft drinks aboard for sale, or you can pack a lunch. Bring a sweatshirt even in summer, and winter gear at other times. Whale watches cost $30 for adults and $20 for children twelve and under. Seal and eagle watches are $20 for adults and $15 for children. Family or other groups of ten or more get a discount. Reservations are recommended so that the captain can call you if a cancellation due to bad weather is necessary; no deposit is required. Call 443–7259.

On Route 213 off I–95 or Route 1, **Harkness Memorial State Park** is on the seaside site of a former private estate, with a mansion currently undergoing restoration as a museum. The park itself is a feast for the eyes, and the summer concert series held here in July and August is food for the soul. Internationally and nationally known performing artists from André Watts to Natalie Cole entertain crowds of music lovers seated or sprawled on the lawn overlooking the sea. There couldn't be a better way to end a tour of New London County than to buy tickets for one of these performances and take a hamperful of bread, strawberries, and cheese to the seaside and soak up the notes. Sadly, these events are not free. Only that would make them better for families.

The park is open year-round. In summer, a parking fee is charged throughout the week; off-season from Labor Day to Memorial Day, no fee is charged. A picnic area and fishing area are offered for day visitors, but no swimming is allowed. For park information, call 443–5725. For concert information, call (800) 969–3400.

GENERAL INDEX

SUBJECT INDEX